CELEBRATING A SMALL ENGLISH GARDEN

A South African's Garden in the Rocky Mountain Region

Published by Bradorlee Press
Golden, Colorado

Bradorlee Press
c/o
Gardens Unlimited
138 South McIntyre Way
Golden, CO 80401

Cover and Interior Design by Carol A. Core, Jane Doe Consulting,
ccore@uswest.net
Photographs by Maureen Jabour
Illustrations by Drew Thurston
Index by Diane Gemmill

ISBN: 0-9705108-0-2

This book printed in Canada

Celebrating

A Small English Garden

For
my husband, Chris,
our children,
Bradley, Dorienne and Lee-Ann,
and grandson, Nicholas.

Celebrating

A Small English Garden

MAUREEN
JABOUR

Photography by Maureen Jabour
Illustrations by Drew Thurston

Bradorlee
Press

Urn with Geranium (*Pelargonium*), verbena (*Tapiens*), *Lobelia erinus*, English ivy

Table of Contents

A private, shady nook is a peaceful setting for afternoon tea.

INTRODUCTION

*W*e lived in South Africa all our lives, as did our parents and grandparents. Our house in Waverley was in an older suburb of Johannesburg. The street names, Argyll, Atholl, Bruce, Knox and Stuart were named by the nostalgic Scotsman who had owned the farm. South Africans followed the traditional English style of gardening; stone or brick walls, or thick hedges screened the garden from the outside world allowing passersby only tantalizing glimpses through the gate or the driveway of the beautiful interior.

In our garden, brilliantly colored, twelve-foot-tall hibiscus; blue, purple and white yesterday, today and tomorrow (*Brunsfelsia pauciflora*); azaleas and roses were its backbone, while the vines of dazzling bougainvillea, sweetly scented jasmine, and the trumpet shaped flowers of bignonia cherere cascaded over the walls. The beds were filled with red and yellow cannas (*Canna x generalis*), the rounded heads of blue agapanthas (*A. africanus* Lily of the Nile) and the elegant spikes of red-hot poker (*Kniphofia uvaria*). Gazanias, vygies (*Lampranthus roseus*) and Namaqualand daisies (*Dimorphotheca sinuata*) were planted in sunny locations, their glowing colors adding to the visual feast. Pride of India trees (*Lagerstroenia indica*) with their trusses of rose-pink flowers, lined the driveway leading up to the house. Lining the wide streets and creating a canopy of coolness were purplish-blue flowering jacarandas and majestic oak and plane trees.

In the summer, afternoon tea in the garden was a tradition. Friends and their children would pop in for a welcome break of chat and a hot "cuppa" accompanied by freshly baked scones or cake. In the winter, because July was an especially cold month, tea was served indoors with everyone seated around the big kitchen table. For more formal occasions, the tea was held in either the living room or the dining room.

Top:
Mexican aster
(Cosmos bipinnatus)
brightens up a
bed of purple asters
(Aster
novi-belgii 'Daniella').

Bottom:
Goldenrod
(*Solidago*)

In 1979 we emigrated to America, choosing Denver, Colorado as our new home. Denver was recommended to us by an American friend who stressed the beauty of the mountains, the similarity of the weather to that of Johannesburg (minus the snow), and the charm of what was then a small city. We were fortunate in our choice.

What a marvelous hobby gardening is and what joy my small garden has given me and my family. The mystery of course is why we do it. What is it about gardening that so many of us find alluring? Surely it is not going out in a snowstorm to shake a tree free of snow, or in a driving wind to prop up battered perennials? What madness propels us out into a freezing spring morning to check for frost damage? Gardening is one of the most demanding of hobbies, it takes years before we see the fruits of our labor, and with one hailstorm, the garden can be destroyed in minutes. Without the guiding hand of the gardener, the garden will revert in one season to a hodge-podge of chaos. Surely whom the gods wish to destroy, they first make them into gardeners. Despite these dreary facts, gardening can be the most rewarding of occupations. It's the feeling of accomplishment as we view a successful flower bed, it's the pleasure of seeing the first clematis buds unfurl, it's the heady rapture of contemplating the luscious buds of a favorite rose. These are the delights that make gardening so worthwhile. The mastery of this hobby is within the grasp of anyone who is enthusiastic and who is willing to learn. As my mother and grandmother used to say "practice makes perfect" and "patience is a virtue." The educated gardener is one who knows how to find out what he or she doesn't know. The paucity of my knowledge can at times be a humbling experience, especially when I sourly contemplate a failed project, which on paper had looked so brilliant. Knowledge truly is the mother of perfection. Baronial acres or ducal estates are not necessary in order to create a successful garden. A small suburban lot, a townhouse garden or even a patio container garden can become the canvas on which to paint our artistic dreams.

Carpe diem.

A narrow flagstone path makes it easy to maintain the plants in a deep bed.

Rosa: 'Red Cascade,' white 'Iceberg,' and 'Cherish' roses combine for a lovely display all summer long.

Chapter One

Hired in Haste, repented at Leisure

Incompetent Landscapers

When visitors view my garden they can't begin to understand the difficulties involved and the length of time it took (ten years) for it to reach the present state of maturity. As a recent immigrant from South Africa, I relied on word-of-mouth recommendations for contractors which were usually reliable. The house was built on a barren, steep slope; retaining walls would have to be built before a garden could be contemplated. Several people told me that Waylon was an excellent rock wall builder who had built walls in adjacent suburbs. When I spoke to him, the extravagant claims he made of the massive walls he had built strained credulity to the utmost, but still I decided to go ahead. That he and his team were wall builders was never in doubt, whether the walls remained standing was quite another story. I rushed on madly to my doom. He arrived one morning in his truck; he was a large man of considerable girth, wearing capacious overalls of ancient lineage, one strap of which was held with a safety pin. A battered cowboy hat cocked at a jaunty angle completed the outfit. His manner was amiable, his smile toothy, though missing a bicuspid. He exuded an air of confidence and bonhomie. He inspected and measured the area and quoted a reasonable price. He pocketed the down payment. It was arranged that half the rocks would arrive the next Monday to be followed in the morning by the rest of the material and the crew.

On Tuesday morning I stood, filled with hopeful expectation, on the sidewalk. My thoughts were interrupted by a strange noise coming from the bottom of the hill; it was not quite a screech, nor was it a whine, it was more like the sound of a machine being tortured. Wheezing and backfiring, and attended by a belching plume of smoke, it resolved itself into a 1950's Chevrolet. It clanked and clattered as it shuddered on balding tires to a shaky stop. Several vital parts were missing: the front bumper, one windscreen wiper and the left back window. Up to the halfway mark it was painted a brownish-rust color, which, on closer inspection proved to be rust. Boxes and/or parcels covered in a tarpaulin were lashed by ropes and string to the top of the car; they looked more complicated to untie than the Gordian Knot.

A scruffy dog of indeterminate parentage was the first to emerge. It immediately staked its claim to the small patch of front lawn (installed a few weeks previously) by liberally spraying around the spindly tree (my pride and joy), and the few spiraea bushes. It completed its toilette by sitting down and inspecting its hindquarters in unseemly detail. During the interminable time it took to complete the project, a faulty burglar alarm in a neighbor's house would go off periodically. This was the signal for the wretched quadruped to interrupt whatever activity he was engaged in—searching for fleas, chasing his tail and other muttlike diversions too indelicate to mention in a gardening book—by throwing his head back and howling mournfully. He sounded uncannily like the Hound of the Baskervilles.

The team was a family affair, an interesting mix of Waylon's two sons, a nattily-dressed cousin encased in jeans so tight they were in imminent danger of splitting, two uncles and a gnarled old man whose relationship was never made clear; he did most of the work.

Thus assembled, the team spread itself out next to the dog and waited for Waylon's arrival; they waited in vain. To pass the time, they turned on their radio, which though somewhat battered, was still able to produce an alarming level of sound. The calm of the neighborhood was shattered by the hideous shrieking of rock stars mouthing gibberish and the infernal din of wailing electric guitars. Three hours later, with the instrument of torture raging on unabated, the team piled back into the vehicle, the engine was fired up, and amidst grating gears and a few hiccups, it disappeared down the hill, a section of tarpaulin flapping wildly.

Scattered on my once pristine scrap of lawn were empty soda cans and crumpled packets of cigarettes, the butts of which had been gathered into a neat pile. A half-eaten, slightly discolored hotdog rejected by the mutt had been thrown into the bushes. To calm my jangled nerves, I went into the house and made myself a nice cup of tea. It was not an auspicious start to the project. Nobody appeared for the rest of the week, although a hopeful sign was the delivery of another pile of rocks. My Financial Backer, who also was the gentleman with whom I'd walked down the aisle all those years ago, became restive if not downright crotchety, a sure prelude to a serious bout of nagging and whining. It was not my finest hour.

I phoned Waylon. His wife answered and told me that the whole crew (and presumably the hound), had gone urgently to repair a fallen wall in Fort Collins. She was a chatty woman who soon treated me to an unwelcome account of the intricate workings not only of her intestinal tract, but also the malfunction of one major organ.

The following Monday morning I heard the sweet sound of the Chevrolet gasping and laboring up the hill; hard on its heels, came Waylon in the truck with implements and the seventh member of the team. This was a brother-in-law, who, to the best of my knowledge did nothing the entire time he graced my property with his presence. He spent his time leaning on a spade and gazing thoughtfully into the middle distance. The nattily dressed cousin was his rival in indolence, busying himself with scraping mud off his polished boots, sitting in the sparse shade of the tree smoking cigarettes or lazily teasing the dog. Promptly at two o'clock the cousin would retire to the car to take a nap. This was because he stayed up late "partying," the uncle confided in me.

He had to catch up on his sleep. The snores and grunts issuing from the car amply affirmed this statement. All, except the little old man and one son, seemed to work at an agonizingly slow pace.

During the following months, whenever I glanced out of the window, a scene of bustling inactivity met my eyes. The cousin, who it appeared was in charge of the victuals, would unpack a seemingly endless supply of substantial meals; the hound would be either scratching frantically in his nether regions or snapping at the flies buzzing around his ears, and the brother-in-law would be joined by one of the uncles in their leaning-on-the-spade routine. It was a depressing sight and not one I recall with affection.

By the end of the sixth week so much progress had been made that even the Financial Backer was able to produce a few wintry smiles and some gracious words of approval. However, I found the slowness of the pace excruciating, especially when several times sections of the wall fell down. Surely Hadrian's Wall had been built in a shorter time?

At the end of three months the last stone was heaved into place and the final inspection took place. The wall did look impressive, though to my untutored eye it seemed to bulge in several areas. Waylon assured me that this was to be expected as the foundation stones still had to settle. Strangely, his optimism failed to reassure me.

The final payment was pocketed; the crew tightened the ropes more firmly around the tarpaulin (what was in it?) then arranged themselves in the car with the dog - but not before he had deposited an inordinately large turd under the hapless tree. With the little old man driving, the machine was started. It lurched forward and the engine died. The crew, with exception of the driver, the nattily dressed cousin and the dog, got out and pushed. The engine caught, a small cheer went up and they scrambled back into the contraption. Amidst billowing smoke and attended by diverse rattles, it disappeared down the hill for the last time.

The Financial Backer's prediction that the wall would fall within a month was unfounded; it fell down after a heavy rain the second month. A frantic call to Waylon proved fruitless as it was answered by an adenoidal youth whose grasp of the English language was rudimentary. From his garbled account, I learned that the crew was on an extended vacation, while Waylon and his wife (accompanied by her digestive tract and major organ) were touring a National Park in the brother-in-law's motor home. The date of their return was uncertain.

I decided to look on the bright side. No longer would I have to experience the dread as the crew's radio was hauled out of the car; nor would I have to gaze at the depressing sight of the uncle relaxing in the wheelbarrow and lighting up yet another cigarette; nor would I have to contemplate the damage done to the shrubs by the incessant squirtings of the four-footed one.

CHAPTER TWO

"IT'S BETTER TO HAVE PLANTED AND LOST
THAN NEVER TO HAVE PLANTED AT ALL."

Patience is a Virtue

As a South African immigrant I had to learn about the different perennials and the vagaries of the weather of the Colorado foothills. My half acre garden (zone 5/4) was started from scratch in 1986 on what was an inhospitable site. The scene confronting me that first March was worse than dreary, it induced a deep gloom. It was a landscape of unrelieved desolation; it made the Sahara Desert look inviting. The north and east sides were hideous with a ten foot slope to the boundary, and as there were no trees, the lack of privacy was astonishing. Snow still lay on the ground as I skipped out to survey this wasteland—well, not actually skipped, more of a shuffle and a slither. After the disaster of the rock wall the previous year, I decided to divide the garden into eight sections, doing one section a year and by subcontracting, I was able to oversee every aspect of my plan. Every spring for the next ten years the same ritual would repeat itself. A large truck loaded with implements, flagstone, sand and workmen would arrive and disgorge itself on the sidewalk. Staring despondently out of the window at the frenzied activity, the gentleman with whom I reside, (my husband also doubles as a part-time

Above: Under a north facing deck, a drab area is transformed by filling pots of different sizes with impatiens and begonias. The fronds of a fern provide contrast.

Below: Rosa: Yellow 'Sunsprite' and Pink 'Simplicity'

Gardening Assistant) would bleat pathetically that he thought that the garden was finished. Hadn't I told him last year that the garden was finished? In heaven's name when was the damn garden going to be finished? Assuming an air of confidence which I had all too little reason to feel, I would assure him that this year was the final lap, yet knowing what vicissitudes still lay ahead. As each project was completed I rushed to the nursery to buy plants.

Tempus fugit; this spring was the first in which no large truck appeared; the sidewalk remained free of shovels, wheelbarrows and workmen. The look of dread did not mar the face of the One Who Bleats. Calm reigns; the garden is finished....I think....yet what about that irritating eyesore under the deck? Maybe next year?

Right:
Clematis
'Ernest Markham'

Rosa: 'Carefree Wonder'

Chapter Three

ASK NOT FOR WHOM THE GARDEN BLOOMS,
IT BLOOMS FOR THEE

All the Garden's a Stage

ost of us develop an interest in gardening when we are confronted with our first piece of land. We should view the garden as a stage and like Cecil B. de Mille we will be directing a cast of thousands. Some of these actors can at times be temperamental, therefore the gardener-as-director should always be in control, and ultimately is responsible for whether the curtain goes up on a brilliant success or a boring flop. As the players take the stage, the director must decide whether a dramatic entrance is required or whether a more muted performance is called for. Certain roles might be enlarged or dispensed with. An actor might become ill; the resourceful director will have understudies waiting in the wings ready to step in. If unreliable actors are retained, the production could be jeopardized.

In my garden, the day lily "Stella d'Oro" was the undependable actor. Assurance by many experts that it was a prolific bloomer proved to be depressingly inaccurate; indeed, its performance was so pathetic it was ushered off the stage amid boos and hisses. Props on the stage should be appropriate; phony looking or kitschy scenery can detract from the overall picture. In the garden these props such as ornaments, fountains, statues and urns should complement the tout ensemble; unsuitable objects would introduce a jarring note into an otherwise harmonious scene. The backdrop, trees, hedges, walls and fences, all add to the success of the production, culminating in a standing ovation and requests for an encore. I have made many mistakes: they throb in the memory like an old injury.

Remembrances of things past are not always pleasant. The only panacea (if it's not too expensive) is to correct the mistakes promptly. He who hesitates is not only lost, but will be condemned to gibber with rage every time the egregious error is viewed.

In mid-summer, this large bed is dominated by the different yellow shades of yarrow (*Achillea* 'Moonshine') false sunflower (*Heliopsis helianthoides*), marigolds, and the white splash of shasta daisies (*Leucanthemum x superbum*). Edgings of blue *Lobelia erinus*, red dianthus and verbena provide the contrast. The background of tallhedge (*Rhamnus frangula* 'Columnaris') adds depth and vertical interest. *Clematis* 'Ernest Markham' scrambles up the wall.

In the front of the house, between the driveway and the lawn, is a ten foot by eighteen foot island bed edged with xeriscape plants, lambs' ears (*Stachys byzantina*), catmint (*Nepeta*) and thyme. A honey locust in the center of the bed has grown to 30 feet and gives dappled shade to the driveway. Against the house is a seven foot by forty foot border. Two Japanese tree lilacs soften the severity of the bricks, while two tallhedge buckthorn (*Rhamnus frangula* 'Columnaris') and three golden vicary privet (*Ligustrum x vicaryi*) provide vertical interest. A dwarf Alberta spruce (*Picea glauca* 'Conica') stands guard on one side of the bed. This adorable evergreen with its dense whorls of green retains its conical shape without shearing. Planted twelve years ago it is now ten feet high and its girth is decidedly plump. Its only requirement is a protected position out of the dry winter winds. It is attractive in all seasons, but is especially so in spring when new light green growth emerges.

These large beds (there are six more throughout the garden) are colorful from spring until frost, as each wave of carefully selected perennials makes its entrance, dominates the stage, then gracefully bows out. The following perennials are repeated in most of the beds: yarrow (*Achillea* 'Moonshine'), shasta daisies (*Leucanthemum x superbum*), goldenrod (*Solidago*), *Aster x frikartii*, New England aster (*Aster nova-angliae*), obedient plant (*Physostegia*), black-eyed Susan (*Rudbeckia fulgida*), *Sedum spectabile* 'Autumn Joy' and *Boltonia Asteroides* 'Snowbank.' Deliciously perfumed English lavender (*Lavandula augustifolia*) should have a home in every garden. Spring is heralded by tulips—I love the bunch-flowering 'Georgette' series, grape hyacinths (*Muscari*), and *Anemone coronaria* ('De Caen'). They are complemented by basket of gold (*Aurinia saxatilis*) and the dazzling white candytuft, a plant that behaves with exemplary decorum. The glowing profusion of Jupiter's beard (*Centranthus ruber*) is the perfect sun-

Island Bed Mid-Summer
Yarrow (*Achillea* 'Moonshine'),
snapdragons, *Coreopsis* 'Sunray,' shasta daisies

loving perennial starring in all the beds, for it bridges the gap between late spring and the main summer burst of color. It should be staked firmly, otherwise it is inclined to sprawl indolently. The well-behaved Russian sage (*Perovskia*), its lavender flowers floating above gray foliage, and hyssop (*Agastache rupestris*) are planted in semi-dry areas. I'm especially partial to pinks (Dianthus family) for edging. Teamed with aubreta, rock cress (*Arabis*) and pansies, they assure me of an ever-changing palette. Working in the garden, I'm amazed at the activity in the beds: ladybugs bustling about importantly as they devour aphids; plump bumblebees, their bottoms waggling cheekily as they nuzzle into the snapdragons; humming-birds, their wings whirring excitedly as they hover over the honeysuckle. Butterflies wafting around too, add to the summer of my content. Unfortunately, I also see loathsome slugs, and they have the impertinence to copulate brazenly before my horrified gaze. Well! I soon put a stop to that nonsense with a handy pair of scissors.

Rosa: 'Ballerina'

Above:
Rosa:
'Carefree
Delight'

Below:
Rosa:
'Iceberg'
'Regensberg'
'Showbiz'

The piéce de résistance of the back garden is the six foot by thirty foot rose bed backed by a six-foot lattice fence up which three clematis scramble: 'Jackmanii', 'Ville de Lyon' and 'Hagley Hybrid.' They provide a dramatic background for the roses. While I am not a rose expert, I have, over the years, through trial and error, eliminated those prima donnas who took center stage, bloomed, languished and then died. Floribundas and shrub roses have been rewarding for all they require in the spring is pruning, a dollop of slow release fertilizer (Osmacote) and a sprinkling of Epsom salts lightly dug in. I disbud every day (I'm lying, sometimes three times a day), and water only in the morning.

Devoting a bed exclusively to roses can be immensely rewarding. There is only one problem. No matter how large the bed, there is never enough space for every rose one covets. The pleasure of viewing a rose bed is equaled only by the joy of snipping a few stems for an arrangement for the house or for friends. The single stem of a floribunda in a bud vase needs no embellishment; nature has arranged it perfectly.

The following rules should be followed when planning a rose bed;

1. The bed should receive at least six hours of sunshine a day.
2. It should have good drainage.
3. Make sure there are no invasive roots from trees or shrubs.
4. It helps to have an indulgent partner; roses are expensive.

If the bed is deep and against a wall, leave some space at the back. The narrow path allows the gardener to work comfortably without compacting the soil; or if possible, create an island bed allowing access from all sides.

The ideal time to prepare a bed – digging, then applying copious amounts of manure, compost and peat – is in the fall, or a month before planting in the spring. This allows the soil to settle and will prevent air pockets from forming.

Even though it might be more expensive, plants should be bought from a reputable source. My Assistant Gardener's suggestion that I buy from a nursery whose flyer arrived in the mail, was ignored.

"DARLENE'S TWO-BIT, DIRT-CHEAP GARDEN EMPORIUM.
ROSES! ROSES! ROSES! 75% OFF!
HURRY WHILE SUPPLIES LAST!!
FREE BALLOONS WITH PURCHASE!"

The attached map showing the route we would have to travel – through creeks, several counties and over mountain passes (though skirting Afghanistan) – to reach Darlene's Emporium took the edge off the Assistant Gardener's enthusiasm. He mourned, though, the loss of that huge discount.

If space in the garden is limited, a few roses can be incorporated successfully into a perennial bed. 'Bonica', 'Iceberg' or 'Simplicity' planted at the back of the bed complements blue and purple perennials such as *Salvia officinalis* (sage), English lavender, or *Geranium* 'Johnson's Blue' (cranesbill). An edging of dianthus alwoodii, which will bloom for most of the summer if deadheaded, would complete a charming picture.

The following are disease-resistant, hardy floribundas and shrub roses which have excelled in my garden:

'Ballerina' – Shrub; tall; single pink; clusters resemble a dancer's tutu

'Bonica' – Floribunda; medium /tall; salmon-pink; glossy green foliage

'Carefree Delight' – Shrub; tall; clusters of single, pink flowers; thorny

'Carefree Wonder' – Floribunda; medium; pink with a splash of white; slight fragrance

'Cherish' – Floribunda; medium; salmon-pink; glossy foliage; slight fragrance

'Gene Boerner' – Floribunda; tall; pink; glossy foliage; slight fragrance

'Iceberg' – Floribunda; tall; white; light green foliage; few thorns; sweet fragrance

'Regensberg' – Floribunda; medium; brilliant pink/white edging; moderate fragrance

'Showbiz' – Floribunda; low/medium; scarlet; slight fragrance

'Simplicity' – Floribunda; tall; shell-pink; light green foliage

Rosa: 'Carefree Wonder'
'Showbiz,' 'Cherish'
'Iceberg'

The steep west slope has been converted into a gorgeous setting with ten steps, side pockets, and an eight by fourteen foot planter. This project took two years to complete; the final result more than compensates for the aggravation and hard work it entailed. I decided to have round edged steps that widen as they descend as I feel they have a more pleasing visual appeal; a three-foot wide landing was incorporated at the halfway mark which induces one to pause and admire the planter, half of which is in shade. Ferns, astilbe, bleeding heart (*Dicentra*), goats beard (*Aruncus*), and lashings of impatiens thrive here.

Timber walls corrected the steep north slope. The Assistant Gardener watched from the window with mounting horror as a mountain of fill dirt was trucked in. He cringed as each wheezing truck-load approached and gloomily predicted disaster. "Mark my words," intoned the Voice of Doom, "this whole damn thing is going to collapse. Now don't say I didn't warn you." Like Pontius Pilate he washed his hands of the whole affair. Until the completion of this particular project, discontented rumblings would erupt with monotonous regularity from his corner.

The weeks passed for me in an agony of apprehension, but gradually, I was happy to see that the years of planning had paid off. At the end of each project I resembled the general appearance of someone who had spent the night outdoors on the compost heap. The night that the final project was finished I went to bed suffused with the glow of a job well done. However, every silver lining has a cloud, and small mistakes had to be rectified. Each minor correction was accompanied by the anguished squawks of the distraught Assistant Gardener, who complained bitterly that the Hanging Gardens of Babylon had taken less time to complete.

Large trees were planted on the north lower level while a lattice fence was installed on the upper level. This fence ends in an "L." In the alcove created by the fence is a wooden bench backed by a

The stone bench is a good place from whcih to view the rose bed.

clematis 'Jackmanii.' This area is an invitation to sit and admire the variety of plants. The graceful branches of a cut leaf maple (*Acer saccharinum*) 'Wierii' give welcome shade. The patio looks onto this area and the main lattice bed. The clematis 'Bees Jubilee' has pride of place here, as well as two roses, 'Regensberg' and 'Carefree Wonder.' The remainder of the bed is a merry mélange of *Crocosmia* 'Lucifer,' *Heliopsis helianthoides*, shasta daisies and goldenrod (*Solidago*).

A formal tea on the patio is enhanced by the courtyard, while the gurgling of a stone fountain adds to the tranquillity.

To garden successfully, one needs a dollop of humility, a smidgen of good luck and a soupçon of commonsense: the rest is hard work.

Three circular flagstone steps flanked by two urns lead down to the rose bed. A stone bench on one side is the perfect spot to sit peacefully and admire the roses and the cascading clematis. Honeysuckle (*Lonicera* "Scarlet Trumpet") grows on one side of the fence (the humming birds love this climber); on either side two stone troughs are ablaze with dianthus, *Lobelia erinus* and alyssum. As one strolls around this once dreary area, it is difficult to imagine the transformation that has taken place over the years.

Aphids

There is nothing more annoying than finding the buds and stems of the roses covered with those minute pests—aphids. I deal with them not by using insecticide sprays, but by relying on the gardener's best friend, the ladybug. If there is a paucity of them in the garden, perhaps because of severe winter cold, they can be bought in mesh bags from the nursery. The bags should be kept out of the sun until the late afternoon. This is the best time to scatter them. They will go to work immediately with amazing efficiency. Another effective method is to rub the buds and stems of the roses gently between forefinger and thumb. Dislodging and squashing the aphids is a tedious operation, but it can also give the gardener immense satisfaction as the buds are cleaned of these voracious insects.

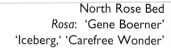

North Rose Bed
Rosa: 'Gene Boerner'
'Iceberg,' 'Carefree Wonder'

CHAPTER FOUR

To plant is human—to succeed divine

Practice Makes Perfect

ardening is an activity in which one's knowledge and patience is constantly tested. Invaluable aids to the accumulation of this knowledge are experimenting in one's own garden and wide reading. No garden can be created in a year, there is no such thing as an instant garden. The impatient gardener who tries to achieve too much in a short space of time will soon feel overwhelmed and will become discouraged. A hobby which should be an enriching experience will become tedious. Anyone thinking of introducing flower beds into their garden should start with one or two manageable beds. Then the gardener can ascertain whether these are easy to cope with and whether more should be added the following year. This is how a garden should evolve.

While a perennial bed might look as though it has been put together haphazardly, it actually happens over several years by experimenting, and with careful planning and discipline. This is especially true if the gardener wants color and variety from spring until frost. Timing of bloom and height are of paramount importance. It is fairly easy to have a one-month bed of, for example, a magnificent display of day lilies or perhaps shasta daisies: it is more challenging to achieve a longer period of bloom. The anticipation of each month's crop of different flowers is what makes perennial gardening a joy.

Clematis 'Jackmanil'
'Ernest Markham'

Two wide, shallow flagstone steps lead one down from the front garden onto the lawn of the narrow (twenty two feet) east side. The wooden posts of a small deck are festooned with clematis 'Nelly Moser' and 'Comtesse de Bouchaud.' Nelly is happy with this position receiving only morning sun. Although both these clematis have mauve-pink flowers, Nelly blooms earlier while the Comtesse takes over to ensure a longer period of bloom. This east area is divided by an iron fence, the gate of which opens onto the back garden. Scrambling up this fence are two clematis, 'Jackmanii' and 'Ernest Markham.' From the gate one looks onto the main bed which is twelve feet by eighteen feet. The centerpiece of this deep bed is a classic stone urn on a pedestal. It is flanked by two upright junipers which over the years have been shaped into lollipops. A Colorado blue spruce (*Picea pungens glauca*) and two pinyons (*Pinus edulis*) provide a dramatic backdrop for the urn and the flowers. In the shady part of the bed, ferns, astilbe and bleeding heart (*Dicentra*)

Clematis 'Nelly Moser'

Previous pages:
Urn flanked by
Helenium autumnale,
Heliopsis helianthoides,
black-eyed Susan
(*Rudbeckia fulgida*)
and cosmos

flourish, while the front of the bed is crammed with Valerian, Jupiter's beard, *Heliopsis helianthoides,* *Helenium autumnale,* shasta daisies, *Rudbeckia fulgida* 'Goldsturm,' *Aster x frikartii* and *Salvia officinalis* (sage). Annuals such as snapdragons, cosmos and zinnias with an edging of lobelia and dianthus

ensures that this bed is lively and luxuriant all season. As this bed was so deep it was difficult to maneuver in it a narrow flagstone path was installed in the center as well as an edging for the front. This makes it easy to reach and maintain the plants. The division between this area and the larger patio section is a narrow bed filled with begonias; in the center is a small stone fountain. The combination of the fountain, urn, lollipops and the dense green background makes a striking ensemble. On one side of the bed is a Korean lilac 'Miss Kim' (*Syringa pubescens*) while on the other side, two aspen trees stand guard.

Korean Lilac
'Miss Kim'
(*s. pubescens*
subsp. patula)

Wooly thyme, dianthus alwoodii, silvermound (*Artemesia*), alyssum
Grass; ponytail grass (*Stipa tenuissima*)

CHAPTER FIVE

IF YOU GIVE GOOD ADVICE, IT WILL NEVER BE REMEMBERED
IF YOU GIVE BAD ADVICE, IT WILL NEVER BE FORGOTTEN

Xeriscape

When I was asked several years ago to write an article on Xeriscape, I was initially taken aback because the concept had never held much appeal. Xeros derives from the Greek word "dry" and "scape" from landscape. No matter how one looks at it, this means dry gardening, which appears to be an oxymoron. However, when I thought about it, I made the surprising discovery that there are certain areas in my garden where Xeriscape ideas had been employed. This was before I had heard the word or had known what it had meant. My problem area was situated on the west side of the house, the upper part of which backs onto the garage wall, while the lower part was a steep slope. This large expanse of lawn required constant watering and was difficult to mow. I re-designed this area with two things in mind, easy maintenance and minimal water usage. i.e. Xeriscape.

Xeriscape I

1.   The lawn, approximately 600 square feet, was removed, as were four sprinkler heads.

2.   Flagstone was installed on the flat section (next to the garage wall) thereby creating a delightful courtyard effect. Various thymes were planted in the crevices of the flagstone and a stone bench and two urns were set against the wall providing a focal point and a peaceful spot from which to view the garden. White painted lattice was fixed to the wall behind the bench. In

Above: Iron basket filled with ivy and verbena, urns with dwarf Alberta spruce
Below: Thyme

the center of the wall a classical stone plaque hangs, while beneath an iron basket filled with ivy and begonias further softens the wall. What was formerly a dull expanse has been converted into a pleasing and interesting feature.

3.   Cutting into the steep slope, steps were constructed using concrete blocks and flagstone. Side pockets filled with thyme, dianthus and rock cress (*Arabis*) spill over the steps.

4.   The rest of the slope is taken up by a two-tiered planter filled with Russian sage (*Perovskia*), *Salvia argentea*, black-eyed Susan (*Rudbeckia*) and yarrow (*Achillea*). One sprinkler is all that is needed to water this entire area. Unwittingly using the principles of Xeriscape I had converted an area of high water usage into one that was colorful and even more interesting.

One of my favorite, larger Xeriscape perennials is Russian sage (*Perovskia*). It is undemanding, disease resistant and requires only a sunny position and hard pruning in the Spring. I planted it in a small bed overlooking the planter, and it has rewarded me every year from mid-summer to frost with clouds of lavender-blue flowers. This invaluable plant can remain in place indefinitely. However, it doesn't take kindly to division.

Russian sage (*Perovskia*) has pride of place at the top of the planter.

Xeriscape II

Most gardeners, when they hear the word Xeriscape shudder delicately and utter cries of dismay or little squeaks of alarm. They picture a wasteland of stones, rocks and other assorted horrors. This misconception is due no doubt to seeing botched attempts or pictures of uninteresting beds. The whole idea of Xeriscape is to cut down on water usage while still maintaining areas of color using hardy plants.

The thoughtful gardener will soon identify those problem areas which are the heaviest users of water. Wind can play havoc with sprinklers. Dry areas will soon announce themselves with the appearance of those irritating brown patches. The dreary ritual of hauling the hose to these affected areas will begin again.

Xeriscape can be charming, elegant or cottagey. Desirable elements of traditional gardening need not be sacrificed at the altar of change if rudimentary rules are followed. Flagstone or concrete pavers interspersed with various thymes and dianthus can be effective whether used as a path or used as a divider between clumps of perennials. A flagstone planter incorporated into the plan can be an element of drama, especially if it is packed with crowd pleasing alyssum, basket of gold, Rocky Mountain penstemon, candytuft and yarrow for spring and summer color. To prolong the season, Russian sage (*Perovskia*) and *Sedum spectibile* 'Autumn Joy' provide a triumphant finale. A stone urn can add an elegant touch, or for a more cottagey look. try wooden tubs overflowing with annual coreopsis and California poppies.

Above
Flagstone squares, thyme,
Silvermound (*Artemesia schmidtiana*)

Right
Silvermound, thyme,
gloriosa daisy (*Rudbeckia hirta*)

Opposite page
Yarrow, Jupiter's beard,
Campanula 'Blue clips'
fill the planter next to the steps.

47

A stone or wooden bench can contribute to the overall charm. Xeriscape is not ripping out the lawn and then dumping a heterogeneous collection of native plants and/or odd looking objects in its place. The forlorn result might resemble Death Valley.

In my front garden, the lawn adjacent to the sidewalk required constant watering. For several years this area had become my pet peeve: I determined to do something about it.

1. The section of lawn 60 feet by 6 feet was removed as well as five sprinkler heads.
2. Cut flagstone 14 inches by 14 inches was laid in a checkerboard pattern.

3. In the empty spaces Xeriscape plants were planted: various thymes, *Veronica liwanensis* (Turkish speedwell), silvermound (*Artemesia schmidtiana*), *Santolina chamaecyparissus*, rock rose (*Helianthemum*) and soapwort (*Saponaria ocymoides*). It took two years for the thyme to knit into a thick mat between the flagstone squares, but it was worth the wait. Last year, English lavender, parsley and oregano were added to the mix, while alyssum, which had seeded itself, created sparkling patches. The flurry of activity and the excitement of the spring and early summer flowering settle down to a calm progression as each square waits its turn to flower. Silky gray silvermound adds restrained color and textural contrast to this delectable company of mainly herbs.

One side of the flagstone squares was attached to the island bed, the front of which was planted with drought tolerant plants. Catmint (*Nepeta*) is an attractive plant which should have a home in every waterwise garden. Its lavender-blue spikes are delightful, and if deadheaded, will obligingly re-bloom. Even when not in bloom, the grey-green mound of foliage provides textural interest and shape. Catmint is inclined to collapse if not supported. I up-end a hanging basket (minus the wires and chains) over it as soon as the foliage starts to emerge. It is said that cats enjoy lounging on catmint. If so, they haven't done any damage to my garden. Perhaps the basket is not a comfortable spot on which to recline.

California poppy and Portulaca seeds were scattered among the crevices. This has paid dividends as their offspring voluntarily appear every year. In the center of this area an old cast iron urn overflows with verbena and lobelia.

Xeriscape is not lolling complacently on your bench all summer, the rules of gardening still apply: namely weeding, deadheading and occasional watering. Whatever "scape" you want to call it, weeds will be indifferent to the changes and will happily re-establish themselves. Although Xeriscape plants, once established, can survive with little water, there are times during exceptionally hot periods when they should be watered. Stressed plants will soon show their displeasure at the lack of attention by sulking, their drooping foliage crying out for moisture. However, they respond quickly and gratefully to minimal care. These rugged plants are survivors. As you survey what had been a dismal wasteland, you can, like Caeser, say "Veni, Vidi, Vici" – "I came, I saw, I conquered that awful space."

Above:
The island bed adjoining the flagstone squares is ablaze with catmint (*Nepeta*), thyme, yarrow and *dianthus deltoides*

Left:
Alyssum, silvermound, Thyme
Grass; *Stipa tenuissima*
Dianthus alwoodii

Below:
Sea thrift (*Armeria maritima*)
lemon thyme, santolina, parsley

Opposite page:
Basket of gold, candy tuft, creeping phlox

The area adjoining the sidewalk never fails to please. It presents a striking picture whether viewed from the house or by interested passersby. Flagstone squares are irresistible to small children who find them an invitation to play hopscotch. Deer ignore the space; perhaps they find the smell of all the herbs unpleasant.

Basket of gold (*Aurinia saxatilis*), a member of the Mustard family, is a perennial whose burst of bright yellow flowers announces the arrival of Spring. Its requirements are simple; well drained, less fertile soil and moderate water. Because it looks untidy after flowering, it should be sheared back and shaped. It might bravely put out a few more blooms later in the season. It grows well in full sun.

Candytuft (*Iberis sempervirens*) is a hardy, late spring perennial with handsome foliage and dazzling white flowers. Low growing and trouble free, it combines beautifully with basket of gold and late blooming tulips. It grows best in the sun with moderate water.

Creeping phlox (*Phlox subulata*) also is known as moss pink. There is no more cheerful sight than creeping phlox in full bloom. This dear little perennial smothers itself with electric pink, blue or white blossoms. It prefers sun and moderate water.

All three of these perennials are low maintenance, disease resistant and need no extra fertilizer.

Xeriscape Plant Guide
A wealth of information can be found in this book published by the Denver Water and American Water Works Association. With an introduction by Rob Proctor, it also offers hundreds of illlustrations by noted artists. This book is invaluable to anyone interested in waterwise plants.

CHAPTER SIX

FOR DUST THOU ART AND UNTO DUST THOU SHALT RETURN.
HEEDETH THIS WARNING BEFORE IT'S TOO LATE,
PLANTETH A GARDEN YOU DON'T WANT TO WAIT.

Garden Ornaments

he ornaments in the garden should be a reflection of one's taste. The creativity of the gardener can be given free rein in the selection of urns, pots, fountains, benches and statues. The correct placement of these objects can transform an ordinary area into a conversation piece, highlight a pretty bed or add a touch of mystery to a wooded background. They should subtly blend into their surroundings. As one glances through the pages of pricey real estate magazines which feature multi-million dollar properties, it becomes clear that some owners show a remarkable lack of taste but a prodigious amount of extravagance; this poor taste is exceeded only by the ostentation with which it is displayed. Those of us with smaller properties know that it is better to choose with care and strive for an understated effect. To avoid the pitfalls of buying unsuitable, pretentious objects, study photographs of gardens in the better magazines, then try to imagine the bench, statue or urn in different areas of your garden. The care and thought given to the decorating of the interior of the house should carry over into the furnishing of the garden. Think and plan before you buy, for unwise and expensive mistakes might haunt you for years: only death will relieve you of the obligation of having to view them every time you venture into the garden. If possible, small children should not accompany you on buying trips. Children have notoriously bad taste. Instead of the divine container you set out to buy, you might be inveigled into purchasing a carload of grotesque gnomes, pink flamingoes or other kitschy knick-knacks. As Shakespeare keeps asking, "What's in a gnome?" The answer is, not much, especially if its face leers evilly at you from the undergrowth. Taking friends with you on these expeditions also can be an exercise fraught with danger. Too many varied opinions and advice can be confusing especially if you're buying an expensive item. You might find yourself gazing onto your small suburban lawn at a massive urn more suitable for the Palace at Versailles. Avoid friends who use the word "cute" to describe gargoyles or any other garden ornament. This is a word appropriate only for babies, puppies or newly hatched chicks. On a recent visit to an outdoor exhibition of garden ornaments this odious word was applied to every hideous plaque, questionable looking animal, plastic windmill and simpering cherub. I went home suffering from a surfeit of "cuteness."

CONTAINERS

Of all the garden ornaments, containers can be the most satisfying way to express one's artistic leanings. They can transform a drab section of the garden or brighten an apartment balcony. Vast acres and a deep purse are not needed for this hobby. Large containers are indispensable for use as focal points to create height, while the smaller ones are useful for moving around or filling in seasonal gaps in the beds. Various containers grouped imaginatively can have an immediate impact on a bare concrete path or patio. While large urns, pots or wooden tubs should be positioned with care to ensure the best visual effect (and once placed are difficult to move), smaller pots can be constantly re-arranged to suit a gardener's whim. The advantage of large containers is that they allow the gardener to create bold, lavish designs and if planted with a long term shrub can provide year-long interest.

Grouping containers by their various heights and planting each one differently allows the viewer to appreciate each separate planting scheme. For example, a large urn (twenty by eighteen inches wide) with a center-

piece of either clipped Rosemary or a small dwarf Alberta spruce with verbena (tapiens) cascading over the sides is lovely. If you surround this with smaller pots of different designs overflowing with seasonal annuals, the effect could be stunning. Smaller pots of 12 inches or less are more effective if planted with one type of annual such as lobelia or alyssum (*Lobularia maritima*). Large containers lined up and planted uniformly make a striking and useful boundary marker; this method also could be used to break up bare expanses of wall. Garage sales and second hand shops can turn up a surprising number of quirky and unusual containers. Old tin buckets, milk pails and

watering cans, for example, with holes drilled in the bottom for drainage would make an interesting centerpiece for a cluster of pots. Daisy-like flowers such as gloriosa daisy (*Rudbeckia hirta*) or *Coreopsis* 'Sunray' create a more informal look.

Above:
Wooden tub with petunias, geraniums and verbena

Below:
A cluster of pots planted with margurite, lobelia and begonias adds interest to a path.

Opposite Page
Above:
Pots with lobelia, coreopsis and alyssum

Below:
Wooden barrels filled with blue, purple and lilac
Lobelia erinus

Front Doors

Two containers, (wooden tubs, urns or large pots) placed on either side of the front door can convey an impression of casual charm, understated elegance or contemporary stylishness. Match them to the facade of the house and the size of the doors. New clay or terra cotta pots can be given a patina of age by rubbing the outside surface with plain yoghurt.

Balconies

On an apartment balcony a sense of summer can be evoked by clustering pots of various sizes and filling them with your favorite annuals and perennials. Use restraint if space is limited, otherwise the result might be too cluttered. On a sunny balcony, a larger pot could comfortably hold a miniature rose. "Holy Toledo" is a deep apricot with adorable buds and a slight fragrance. Perennials such as English lavender (*Lavandula augustifolia*), marguerite (*Anthemis tinctoria*) and *Scabiosa caucasica* (pincushion flower) all add to the vibrant scene. Or what about a herb garden starring *Salvia officinalis* (sage), thyme, mint, parsley and oregano? This would be a visual feast for the senses as well as the table. If the balcony is north facing a delightful arrangement would be an array of pots filled with jewel-like impatiens or begonias. Ferns and hostas incorporated into this shady scheme would add a textural contrast.

Right:
A centerpiece of tallhedge (*Rhamnus frangula* 'Columnaris') rimmed with lobelia, fills an urn

Opposite Page
Above:
Alyssum and verbena spill over the edge of a stone urn.

Below:
At the front door, a stone urn overflows wtih petunias, alyssum and verbena. Two small pots contain lobelia, alyssum and begonias.

For a more formal, sophisticated effect, two or three large urns (fiberglass is lighter, as well as being safer, on a wooden balcony) could be lined up against the outer wall of the balcony. Try an upright juniper sheared to retain a narrow column or clipped balls of boxwood as a centerpiece. Any cascading plant enhances the effect. What an elegant and pleasing sight this would be when viewed from indoors.

Vegetables

Certain vegetables will grow happily in pots - another boon for the sunny balcony. Voracious slugs and their equally repulsive brethren are less prevalent on container grown vegetables. Either buy plants from the nursery or sow the seeds directly into the pots after all danger of frost is past. Pinch out to avoid overcrowding. Successive sowings will give you months of lettuce (Buttercrunch), spring onions and radishes. While you might not be able to feed a horde of ravenous guests with this modest output, it will still give you a feeling of accomplishment as you snip a lettuce and spring onions for a fresh salad. Admittedly, not a Lucullan feast, but nonetheless intensely satisfying.

Tips for Container Gardening

1.   Containers must have adequate drainage. Place a few small stones over the drainage hole to prevent soil seepage.

2.   Mix half Cow and Compost, half potting soil, fill pot to within a few inches of the top of the pot.

3.   The plants should be well watered before planting. Pinch any flowers or buds to encourage bushiness. Plant in the cool of the evening.

4.   After planting, sprinkle several teaspoons of Osmacote or any slow-release fertilizer. Water gently but thoroughly and every morning and evening during hot spells.

5.   Deadhead religiously, it only takes a few minutes every day, but your plants will repay you with a prolonged and prolific period of bloom.

Left: A cast iron pot with verbena and lobelia. Clipped rosemary is the centerpiece.

Opposite page
Above: Against a background of clematis, 'Jackmanii,' a wooden bench is an invitation to sit and relax. The dense branches of a pinyon (*Pinus edulis*) adds to the sense of enclosure.

Below: A birdbath makes an interesting container

Benches, Fountains, Statues and Plaques

*When it looked good,
it looked very good.
When it looked bad,
it looked horrid*

Benches are perhaps the easiest objects to place in the garden. A bench against an evergreen background, tucked into a secluded corner or placed under a shady tree adds instant character to an area. "Lutyens" or "Giverney" benches are stunning, but expensive. Wooden or park benches are comfortable and should be placed where there is a pleasant view. A stone bench (while not as comfortable) has an undeniable appeal, especially if two medium sized urns are placed on either side; these give a pleasing balance and the effect is enhanced if small, sheared upright junipers are planted in them. This idea is charming in a small courtyard.

Above:
Stone plaque

Right:
Fountain flanked by begonias

A fountain is an expensive addition to the garden and once installed, is difficult to move. Before buying, take into account the scale of the area. Large, regal, three tiered fountains with cavorting cupids or nymphs would be inappropriate in a suburban setting. A fountain need not be large to create a tranquil effect; the soothing trickle from even the smallest one is balm for the spirit. One cannot go far wrong with a wall fountain; in an enclosed space they conjure up images of Mediterranean courtyards or secret Islamic gardens.

Restraint should be used when buying statues or other art. Experts should be consulted as to whether a classical or contemporary theme best suits your garden. A well-positioned statue, birdbath or sundial can add appeal to the look of an area. Plaques, especially those with a classical theme, will break up an otherwise dull expanse of wall or fence. Whether it is a tiny townhouse garden or a spread of acres, the garden will be stamped by the personality of the individual.

Above:
Stone trough with geraniums, petunias and lobelia.

Right:
Cluster of pots containing alyssum, begonias and grass *Rhynchelytrum nerviglume* 'Pink Crystals'

Opposite Page Above:
A stone urn is filled with lobelia and dianthus surrounded by marguerite, marigolds and a background of yarrow.

Below:
Clusters of pots with lobelia and alyssum nicely complement a large urn filled with lobelia and verbena.

Chapter Seven

BREATHES THERE ANYONE WITH A SOUL SO DEAD
WHO WOULD NOT ADMIRE A PERENNIAL BED?

Perennials
A Picturesque Portrait

 ost of us start gardening too late in life. When we are young and sprightly we have too many other interests; the middle years are taken up with furthering our careers and/or raising families, so that by the time we should be hitting our stride, the stride has turned into a totter, bones are creaking and backs are aching: the spirit might be willing but the knees are weak. However, it's never too late to start. Growing older is no more than a bad habit that busy gardeners have no time for.

Procrastinating about doing a project is like looking at a wheelbarrow; nothing will happen until we start pushing. Before embarking on the plan of a new bed (or revitalizing an old one) and before rushing to the nursery and filling a cart with unsuitable plants, it is wiser for the gardener to survey the site for a month, allowing ideas to percolate and take shape. Discard outrageous suggestions from inexperienced though well-meaning friends, map several plans, but above all, read. Pictures of magnificent gardens can be inspiring, with gorgeous photos so seductive that the imagination can run riot: we long to emulate them. Realistically, we ordinary gardeners would find these beds difficult to maintain. But as we study these pictures and the layout of the beds, it is apparent that it is the ideas and not the size that we can incorporate into our plans. Like Hercule Poirot, we must use "the little gray cells."

Digging

Roses are reddish
Violets are blueish,
But they won't grow in soil that's glueish.

Gardening is ten percent preparation and 90 percent perspiration; most of the latter comes from digging. Dry, compacted soil can turn even the most ardent digger into a gibbering wreck, so make sure that the ground is soaked but not soggy. As plants won't grow in glue or cement, generous amounts of compost, cow manure and peat should be added.

If the bed is large, rest every fifteen minutes before irritability and exhaustion sets in. Gardening should be relaxing, not a race to get everything done in the shortest possible time. The tines of the fork should go in the full length, while the ideal depth to be dug should be 12 to 14 inches. When I explained this method of composting and digging to an initially enthusiastic group of friends and relatives, the site became a hive of inactivity. One or two of them busied themselves lackadaisically twirling their forks, but merely fluffing up 1/4 of an inch of soil. I had an uneasy feeling that my popularity was waning.

Left:
Heliopsis helianthoides
(false sunflower)

Opposite Page:
Above:
Astilbe 'Cattelya'

Below:
Geranium 'Johnson's Blue'
(cranesbill)

Now that you have surveyed your area, ascertained the amount of sun it receives, checked for problems with water runoff or tree roots, dug and composted, it is time to plant.

Planting

Before planting, place the plants in the area where the holes are to be dug, then move them around until you're happy with the result. If your container plants have become rootbound, tease out some of the roots and spread them out before filling the hole. Allow three to four feet between each plant; any spaces in between can be filled in with annuals such as snapdragons and marigolds with tall cosmos for the rear and California poppies for the front. Water thoroughly and thrust a screwdriver into the soil daily to see if moisture is reaching the roots. Deep water every few days, as superficial watering every day encourages shallow roots to grow towards the surface, not downward, anchoring the plant firmly.

Care
Dead-heading is important to encourage plants to continue blooming as well as to maintain the bed in immaculate condition. If sheared after blooming, some perennials will re-bloom - yarrow (*Achillea* "Moonshine), *Nepeta* (catmint) and *Centranthus ruber* (Valarian, Jupiter's beard), for example. Immediately eradicate any weeds.

Above: yarrow, shasta daisies, *Heliopsis helianthoides*, marigolds and snapdragons
Background: tallhedge

Opposite Page:
Above: Valerian, Jupiter's beard

Below: yarrow (*Achillea* 'Moonshine'), *Nepeta* (catmint), sage (*Salvia officianalis*)

Staking

A stake in time saves nine, so stake early. Attending to this chore after the plants start to bud is an exercise in futility. I recommend staking most of the taller varieties; Physostegia (false dragonhead) is one of the exceptions which is why it is known as "obedient plant". The alternative is to spend the summer vainly propping up heavily flowering plants with an assortment of sticks and branches which cannot be hidden. Much gnashing of teeth will occur as the frustrating task of making obstinate flower stalks face the right way proves hopeless. The result will be a sorry muddle lying on the ground or a confused mass drunkenly leaning on its neighbors. This contretemps will detract from the appearance of the bed. Once the bed is established with hardy, easy to care for perennials, your confidence will grow and it will be an incentive to experiment with something exotic. Embarking on the project of a perennial bed is rather like committing to marriage. There will be promises to be together through sickness and health; if the relationship is to flourish, constant care must be given. The reward will be an outpouring of joyous color (or affection) that will provide you with an interest in the future. Neglect will result in acrimony and dislike; a parting of the ways will be inevitable.

Left:
Heliopsis helianthoides,
shasta daisies

Opposite Page:
Above:
Sedum spectabile
'Autumn Joy,'
black-eyed Susan
(*Rudbeckia fulgida*
'Goldsturm')

Below:
Aster novae-angliae
'Harrington's Pink,'
black-eyed Susan

Above:
Left: yarrow (*Achilliea* 'Moonshine')

Right: *Coreopsis* 'Sunray'

Opposite page:
Above:
fleabane (*Erigeron*)

Below:
Aster x frikartii 'Wonder of Stafa,' Russian sage
(*Perovskia*)

Sun-Loving Perennials

SPRING

Rock cress (*Arabis*) Showy racemes of pure white adorn the slowly spreading mat. Ideal for rock gardens and xeriscape.

EARLY SUMMER

Centranthus ruber (Valerian, Jupiter's beard) has upright stems bearing fluffy clusters of pink or white flowers. Moderate water. Stake. Grows to height of 2 feet, Divide every two years.

MID-SUMMER

Black-eyed Susan (*Rudbeckia fulgida* 'Goldstrum') has leafy branching stems which become a mass of stunning orange daisies with a black center. Long-flowering, Regular water. Grows to height of 2 to 2 1/2 feet., Divide every two years.

MID-SUMMER

Shasta daisy (*Chrysanthemum x superbum*) makes a spectacular splash of white in a bed. 'Alaska' is tall, 'Marconi' is medium, 'Snowcap' is short. Regular water, Divide every two years.

Coreopsis (tickseed) has charming yellow daisy-like flowers at the end of wiry stems. 'Early Sunrise' blooms a few weeks before "Sunray." *Coreopsis verticillata* 'Zagreb' is shorter. Moderate water, Grows to 2 - 2 1/2 feet, Divide every two years.

Heliopsis helianthoides (False sunflower) is long-blooming, with yellow, single or double flowers. Needs extra water during dry, hot periods. Plant at rear, Grows to 2 1/2 - 3 1/2 feet, Divide every two years.

Boltonia asteroides 'Snowbank' when in bloom has sprays of white, yellow-centered aster-like flowers. Self-supporting, moderate water, Grows to height of 3 feet, Divide every three years.

Sedum spectabile 'Autumn Joy' has sturdy stems, fleshy leaves, and flowerheads that start out pink, then age into a striking bronze. Moderate water, Grows to height of 3 feet, Divide every three years.

Sedum spectabile 'Autumn Joy,' *Aster x frikartii* 'Wonder of Stafa'
Annuals: alyssum, begonias, gloriosa daisy (*Rudbeckia hirta)*
Background: privet (*Ligustrum vulgare* 'Lodense'), (*Juniperus scopulorum* Rocky Mountain Juniper)

Final Tasks

After a dinner party, it's a wise host who, after the guests have left, immediately tackles the task of cleaning up. Leaving this for the morning will result in an unsettled sleep and the dismaying sight of a chaotic kitchen. The same holds true for the garden, where cleaning up and dividing the perennials in the fall is as important as caring for them in the growing season. The best time to renew an established bed is just after the glory starts to dim. Dig deeply around the plants; if there is no shade, cover them with newspapers to keep the roots from drying out. Label them, because once they are removed, identification is difficult. This is a good time to take stock. It makes no sense to keep plants which you have come to loathe in the forlorn hope that your feelings will change. Be ruthless; looking at something which has irritated you all season is unfortunate; re-planting it is folly. Banish it to the outer reaches of Mongolia if necessary, but get rid of it. To err is human; to discard, divine. Dividing root-bound perennials can test anyone's patience. Otherwise calm gardeners have been known to dance around dementedly in an effort to divide obstinate roots. If you have an assistant (my Assistant Gardener, though recalcitrant at times, can be extremely helpful), so much the better. Place two forks back-to-back in the center of the plant and push down, all the while pulling in opposite directions, until the roots loosen. Certain perennials, such as obedient plant and black-eyed Susan should be divided every two years otherwise they are inclined to shoulder their less robust neighbors out of the way. Add compost, cow manure and peat to the well-dug and weeded bed. After discarding and dividing, you will have twice the number of plants with which to start a new bed. Make sure the plants are firmly anchored and water generously every few days until it rains or snows.

Above: candytuft (*Iberis sempervirens*),   Below: *Phlox paniculata* 'Eva Cullum'

CHAPTER EIGHT

THE LESS SAID, SOONEST MENDED,
THE MORE SAID, SOONEST OFFENDED

The Assistant Gardener

hile I design beds, plant, clip, weed and hand water, there are times when I need help. On these occasions I employ the Assistant Gardener who can carry heavy bags with ease, reach up to lop a branch and dig holes for shrubs. As Head Gardener at times I have had to be firm with this employee in the face of outlandish floral design suggestions and to ignore all his unwanted advice. After some initial unpleasant haggling over his salary, we eventually reached a satisfactory sum of remuneration, which also included his meals. An added bonus for me is that he lives on the property. This employee can sometimes be quite impertinent and I have had to exercise my authority and to speak sharply at his refusal to do certain tasks; he also has an irritating habit of sleeping late when specifically instructed to be up early. By and large though, the relationship has been amicable though interspersed at times by demands for a salary increase. Everything in the garden would be rosy except for one drawback; this employee has always collected Stuff. No item has ever been too worn out or valueless that he has felt it should be discarded. From his elevated position as Assistant Gardener he has become an avid collector of Gardening Stuff; he is always on the lookout for gadgets. No advertisement escapes his gimlet eye. It is the extravagant claims made by these advertisements for the removal of weeds that always catches

his attention. The latest contraption, if used correctly can help eliminate deep-seated weeds; unfortunately if wielded by an overzealous beginner, large craters are the unhappy result. Unsuspecting guests and/or the Head Gardener have been known to tumble into these craters. The weeds have disappeared; the chasms remain to lure the unwary to their doom. Strange items have fallen into them, wheelbarrows, shovels and the neighbor's dog. This obnoxious implement has been relegated to the furthest corner of the garage with stern warnings from me as to the misuse of it.

As Head Gardener, I have to be on my guard in order to restrain the Assistant Gardener from adding to his cache of Stuff. I gave the following advertisement (which he was studying raptly) short shrift.

"UNCLE HIRAM'S BARGAIN HARDWARE"
SAVE!   SAVE!   SAVE!
Hurry to Uncle Hiram's
for incredible SAVINGS!
Don't miss these NEW SHIPMENTS!
◆BOXES OF CARPENTER'S NAILS
(slightly bent) 80% OFF!!!
◆ALMOST NEW SPADES & SHOVELS
(Handles need fixing) HUGE DISCOUNT!!
◆FREE lollipops for the kids!

Despite the Assistant Gardener's protests, I treated these exaggerations with the contempt they deserved by tossing Uncle Hiram, his unfixable goods and his lollipops into the garbage.

The Assistant Gardener is unable to throw anything away. He has a heterogeneous collection of bent nails, rusty pieces of wire, shreds of unhygienic-looking rags, battered boxes and broken tools. These are all lovingly and carefully stored away to await the day when they will be needed. Every now and then an inventory is taken of these precious objects and consternation reigns if any of them are found to be missing. Gloom and despondency descend like a pall; the Head Gardener has a decidedly shifty expression. Did some nameless person, while cleaning out the garage come across the missing items and considering them rubbish perhaps thrown them away? Did some intruder steal the handleless saw, hairless brush or the punctured piece of plastic pipe? In short, where the hell is his Stuff? After fruitless and frantic searches in every nook and cranny fails to reveal the whereabouts of the missing items, and when the air has become thick with recriminations and accusations, a dusty box is unearthed from the bottom of a pile of rags. It is greeted with cries of relief and affection and much musing and conjecture as to who had put them there. Harmony has been restored; the Assistant Gardener can get back to work, secure in the knowledge that his Stuff is well hidden and safe from predators.

CHAPTER NINE

CLEMATIS ARE BLUISH, PINKISH, REDDISH
AFTER SOME HAIL, THEY'LL LOOK QUITE DEADISH

Clematis - The Venerable Vine

f the rose is the queen of the garden, then the clematis is surely the queen of the climbers. This plant came into prominence during the reign of Queen Elizabeth the First and was imported to England from the Mediterranean regions and also from China. The colors of this entrancing climber are never gaudy, yet they have a complete range: red, pink, purple, mauve, lavender and white. If well treated, they will bloom with the well bred elegance one would expect from these elites of the climbing world. Clematis belong to the family Ranunculaceae of which there are hundreds of species. It was in the mid-late nineteenth century that this Belle of the Wall became popular in Great Britain; it was in this period that many of todays' favorites were hybridized. Often, they were named for the families or nurseries that bred them. The well known "Jackmanii" was hybridized at Jackman's Nursery in Surrey, while the famous English writer and plantsman William Robinson honored his head gardener with 'Ernest Markham.' In a monastery in Warsaw, Poland, many beautiful clematis have been introduced into the contemporary scene, 'John Paul II.' 'Monte Cassino' and 'Mother Teresa' among others. All over the world experts are experimenting to bring us an even more bewildering selection from which to choose.

The name clematis is derived from the Greek word *klema* which means vine. The correct pronunciation is clem-a-tis, though clem-at-is is also used. Does it matter? For a clematis by any other pronunciation would flower as sweetly and profusely. When I emigrated from South Africa to the less salubrious climate of Colorado I said a sad farewell to the glorious bougainvillea and the sweetly scented jasmine climbers; the lustrous clematis has more than compensated for the loss of those stalwarts, for it is the gardener's best friend, providing a dazzling focal point for any part of the garden. Although it has to be cosseted for a year or two, its color and prolific blooming will assuage the heart of the most despondent gardener. In the spring, it is a rampant grower though it does take a few years before it starts ramping. Plants can be like friends and relatives: some are eagerly awaited and made welcome. However, after a prolonged stay, some become tiresome and one longs for them to go. There are others, like clematis, who delight us, Their arrival is much anticipated, their presence enchants us, their departure leaves a void.

Many of us toy with the idea of planting clematis but are discouraged by all the complicated instructions. To grow them successfully the following simple rules should be followed.

1.   Choose the right site.
2.   Prepare the planting hole well.
3.   Prune (those that need pruning) in the spring.
4.   In the first year never allow the plant to dry out.
5.   In the spring fertilize and guide the tendrils onto their supports.

You will be rewarded with a gorgeous display of shimmering color from this most obliging plant.

Left and opposite above:
Purple 'Jackmanii' and deep pink 'Ernest Markham' provide an appealing combination as they scramble through the iron fences.

Opposite right:
A closer look at the purple perfection of 'Jackmanii'

Above left:
'Jackmanii,' 'Ville de Lyon,' 'Ernest Markham,' and 'Hagley Hybrid' combine to make a brilliant show on a 30 foot lattice fence. They are a dramatic background for the roses. There can be no confusion in Spring as to which plant needs pruning. They are all pruned hard.

Above right:
'Nelly Moser' is an early-blooming charmer, and she prefers afternoon shade. "Nelly" is the ideal clematis for a smaller space.

Choosing the Right Clematis

The different varieties of clematis can be bewildering to the novice. At the nursery, every gardener is allowed to be rash for a short while; prudence dictates that we don't prolong that period. Don't buy the first few plants that take your fancy. Most reputable nurseries have experienced and helpful staff who would be more than willing to guide you. Don't try to hunt down some exotic or difficult-to-find plant that Great Aunt Edith insists you locate when there are an abundance of tried and true favorites available. You'll be joining the sad ranks of the dissatisfied in hot pursuit of the unobtainable. You can't go far wrong with the regal purple of "Jackmanii," the glowing red of 'Ernest Markham' or 'Ville de Lyon,' the shell pink of 'Hagley Hybrid,' the mauve-pink of 'Comtesse de Bouchaud' or the creamy white of 'Henryi.' The American late flowering *C. maximowicziana/panuculata* 'Sweet Autumn' is a vigorous grower which should not be over-looked for its perfume and abundant white flowers.

Above left:
A delightful cascade of 'Ernest Markham,' and 'Hagley Hybrid'

Above right:
'Comtesse de Bouchaud' is an accomodating plant which will happily grow in the sun or sun/part shade.
She is an excellent clematis for growing up a post or pillar.

The flowering period of the clematis will give you a clue as to which site would best suit it. Those that flower in the spring or early summer will thrive in partial shade. Indeed, the mauve flowers of 'Nelly Moser' with its contrasting carmine bars tend to fade if subjected to the fierce rays of the sun. If planted in partial shade (an east exposure is ideal), it will produce brighter colors and will bloom for a longer period. This applies also to 'Bees Jubilee' which is almost a twin of "Nelly." 'Comtesse de Bouchaud' and 'Hagley Hybrid' are versatile and can be planted in sun or sun with some shade. 'Jackmanii,' 'Ville de Lyon,' 'Ernest Markham' and other later flowering species do best in sun. A long wall or fence can be transformed by planting several different colored clematis. Space them four or five feet apart and in several years you will have a stunning wall of color, a sight to captivate even the most blasé onlooker, what a poker aficionado would call a royal flush. If space is limited, two contrasting colors such as 'Jackmanii' and 'Ernest Markham' will intertwine and gracefully festoon an iron or lattice fence. These cascading aristocrats will provide a mantle of sumptuous color for many months. When planting these groups choose those with the same pruning requirements, so that in spring there will be no confusion as to which needs pruning. A good idea too, is to make notes in your gardening journal as to the location of each clematis as you plant them. Include pruning instructions and any other useful information, for the tags will soon be lost. There is nothing more irritating than being confronted in spring with a tangle of dead wood and being unable to identify the different plants.

Opposite and page 82:
Free-flowering best
describes 'Hagley Hybrid.'
The entire plant is covered
from June through August
in shell-pink blooms.

Above:
Late-flowering 'Sweet
Autumn' clematis (*C maxi-
mowiczianapaniculata*) has
an abundance of
tiny white flowers.

Below:
'Bees Jubilee' bears such a
striking resemblance to
'Nelly Moser,' it is difficult
to tell them apart. 'Bees
Jubilee' blooms later than
"Nelly" and prefers some
afternoon shade.

Above left:
A purple mantle of 'Jackmanii' drapes itself over the mailbox. Chicken wire attached to the bricks with nails allows the tendrils to twine firmly around the wire. 'Jackmamii' can grow to twelve feet—the mailbox is five feet. To train the plant over the bricks takes patience. Carefully bend the stems and tie them down with string looped through the chicken wire. The tendrils will soon catch onto the wire.

Above right:
A wall is the ideal place for attaching chicken wire. Here 'Ernest Markham' scrambles up the wall.

Planting

Look for larger plants with plenty of shoots arising from the base. If planted against a wall dig the hole at least one foot away from the wall. The ideal soil is well drained and rich in humus, so add generous amounts of compost, manure and peat to the hole which should measure no less than 20 inches by 20 inches, or twice the width of the container. Bonemeal sprinkled into the forked over bottom of the hole is an added bonus. If the plant is dry, let it stand for ten minutes in a container of water before planting. Remove the plant carefully and make sure that the crown is two or three inches below the soil level. Fill the hole with a mixture of your soil (if good), compost and manure. Sprinkle more bonemeal, then tamp the soil down gently. Leave the supporting cane in and lean it towards the wall. Clematis prefer cool, moist, rich soil, so for the first year keep the roots damp (but not soggy). Drying out is usually fatal. Once established, it will need extra water once a week during prolonged dry periods.

Pruning

Otherwise mild-mannered and dignified gardeners have been known to resort to unseemly squabbling over the contentious issue of pruning. The gentleman to whom I'm closely related by marriage objects to pruning. If left to him the garden would resemble a jungle through which one would have to hack one's way with a machete. While I'm chopping away at the tangled mass he will poke his head out of the door and shake it sadly (the head not the door). The rest of him emerges; he is wearing his gardening clothes, jeans and sneakers - the latter item, of heroic size. "Mark my words," this Voice of Doom glumly intones, "you've killed it. That plant looks as dead as the Dodo." For me, the week following the pruning is an anxious time until the first green shoots appear.

This mystery of pruning is of course easily solved by looking at the tag or asking an expert at the nursery. Group I flowers early and needs no pruning, for they flower on old wood. Groups I I and III should be pruned hard, which means cutting down to approximately one foot and above a healthy pair of buds. Optional pruning applies to those varieties which flower on both old and new wood. All newly planted clematis should be pruned their first spring to encourage bushiness. Contrary to popular opinion, clematis can be moved. This should be done when the plant is completely dormant. Dig a wide deep hole around the plant and re-plant it in a larger hole which has been well prepared with humus and bonemeal. Prune as you normally would in spring and water well. The two five year old plants I moved sulked for the first year, but thereafter have bloomed beautifully. In Colorado it is wiser to delay pruning until all danger of late frost is past because tender shoots are vulnerable to extreme cold.

"The Belle of the Wall"

Above left:
A stone urn filled with *lobelia erinus*, alyssum, dianthus and petunias is nicely complemented by the glowing backdrop of 'Ville de Lyon'

Training

In spring the clematis grows at an astonishing rate, up to one to two inches a day; this is when the tendrils should be guided onto their supports. This task must be carefully done as the tendrils are brittle and can easily break. If they do, don't 'worry too much, this plant is resilient. An intricate birds nest will form if the plant is left to its own devices for more than a week. The most stout hearted gardener will start foaming at the mouth with rage when confronted with this tangled mess; nimble fingers will fail to unsnarl it. To avoid such a contretemps inspect your plants every day or two, although obsessive gardeners will, of course, hover over them every ten minutes. Clematis do not cling to surfaces, they climb by twining their tendrils around their supports. I find that chicken wire is invaluable; it is easy to fix with a few nails to a wall and it is inexpensive, especially if a large area is to be covered.

Enemies

Enemies of the clematis are few, wilt being the most serious for which there is no cure. Fortunately, I haven't yet encountered it. Small insects (which I couldn't identify) attacked "Henryi" last year leaving holes in the perfect flowers. I was like a bride-to-be impatiently waiting for the ring to be produced only to find that it was flawed. This year I will be placing a cut half of grapefruit at his base to attract, then trap these pests; it's worth a try. Hail can be the most damaging. Last year, hail devastated my garden, depleting my usually considerable store of goodwill and stoicism. As I looked towards the mountains the sight plunged me into despondency. As the ominous clouds gathered I felt as though the Sword of Damocles was suspended over the garden. Within five minutes everything was flattened; only the clematis were spared. The common name for clematis is Virgin's Bower named perhaps for the Virgin Mary in Elizabethan England. Was it divine intervention or just sheer good luck? Gardeners can be a superstitious group, (my grandmother would never plant seeds when the moon was waning, my mother would not allow calla lilies into the house) but the more down-to-earth would point out that the plants were protected by the fences and walls. The Duchess of Windsor used to say "You can never be too rich or too thin." To this can be added, "or have too many clematis".

Above right:
When viewed from afar, the deep pink colored flowers of 'Ernest Markham' and 'Ville de Lyon' seem identical. On closer inspection, the difference between them becomes apparent. 'Ernest Markham' has blunt sepals, while 'Ville de Lyon' has an edging of deeper pink.

Above:
'Ernest Markham' and 'Ville de Lyon'

Recommended Clematis

'Bees Jubilee'
Mauve-pink, carmine bars; light pruning; 6-8 feet tall

'Ernest Markham'
Ruby red, blunt tipped sepals, golden stamens; prune hard; 8-12 feet

'Henryi'
Creamy-white, pointed sepals; light or optional pruning; 8-12 feet

'Nelly Moser'
Mauve-pink, carmine bars; light or optional pruning; 6-8 feet

'Ville de Lyon'
Carmine red edged with deep crimson; prune hard; 8-12 feet

'Comtesse de Bouchaud'
Mauve-Pink, cream stamens; Prune hard 6-8 feet

'Hagley Hybrid'
Shell pink, brown stamens; prune hard; 6-10 feet

'Jackmanii'
Purple, prolific bloomer; prune hard; 10-15 feet

'Sweet Autumn' (C maximowicziana/paniculata)
White, star-shaped, fragrant: pruning optional: 15-20 feet

CHAPTER TEN

MARY, MARY, QUITE CONTRARY, HOW DOES YOUR GARDEN GROW?
WITH BUDWROMS, SLUGS AND ALL THOSE BUGS, THERE'S NOT TOO MUCH TO SHOW

Annuals - Gems of the Garden

Every decade has its fashions and fads; these are usually started by an elite clique, who, as soon as the fashion filters down to the masses, discard it as passé. In the Victorian era, bedding plants (i.e. annuals) were all the rage. Regimental rows of plants were de rigueur in every garden. Rigid rows of *Pelargoniums* (geraniums), marigolds and ageratum marched stiffly up and down the beds. These borders were the precursors of the institutional plantings we see today in our parks, street islands and in front of county buildings. In the past many of these designs were spectacularly charmless, uninspired combinations of grey Dusty Miller (*Senecio*), insipid begonias with a centerpiece of raggedy canna lilies. The onlooker was filled with ennui and a longing for the bold contrast of vivid color. Designers today plant dazzling, imaginative beds; brilliant splashes of color which enhance their surroundings whether it be in front of a restaurant or townhouse or at the entrance to a suburban community. Small shops in suburbs fill their urns and containers with gorgeous annuals which lighten the heart of the busy shopper. Pavement cafes have window boxes and containers bursting with a dizzying array of annuals. All these planting ideas can inspire and spur one on to greater efforts in one's own garden. The inflexible Victorian gardening plan was changed when Gertrude Jekyll, the doyenne of English gardeners until her death in 1932, introduced a more imaginative and natural way of using annuals. In her garden designs (several are still in existence), she arranged annuals within the same color wheel. For example, she used various tints of blue and purple or different shadings of pink to great effect. While Vita Sackville-West's white garden at Sissinghurst is world famous, it was Miss Jekyll who first planted a section of garden featuring all silver and white plants; it was a revolution in the art of gardening.

Before embarking on a garden project, the question to be asked is, whether it should be formal or informal. If the garden is small and flat, a formal design is the most visually pleasing and would be the easiest to install. For example, a focal point in the center could be a narrow decorative tree, a small fountain or a sundial. Symmetrical beds on either side should be balanced with the same color annuals such as petunias or *Pelargoniums* (geraniums) and edged with either ageratum or *Lobelia erinus*. This arrangement would be elegant, simple and easy to maintain. If the lot is irregular, an informal design is best. If there are slopes and curves, annual beds could be incorporated into the plan using bolder plantings such as snapdragons, marigolds and bedding dahlias.

Designing beds is best left to one person, for although two heads are sometimes better than one, too many designers can also spoil the bed. My occasional "Partner in Grime," who also is my part-time Assistant Gardener, rather fancies himself as a designer of beds. Certain plants will catch his eye; several years ago it was pampas

Above:
Impatiens, begonias

Below:
Dwarf snapdragons,
Lobelia erinus
and alyssum

Opposite page:
Above:
petunias, *Lobelia erinus*
and marigolds

Below:
Lobelia erinus, begonias

grass and white petunias. At every opportunity he would broach the idea of combining the two. I gently but firmly pointed out the inadvisability of planting a 12 foot tall pampas grass in the middle of a five foot wide bed and surrounding it with white petunias. He was unconvinced and muttered discontentedly for a few days until he was distracted by a new obsession, vegetable gardening. Unknown to me he scattered pumpkin seeds in a flower bed. Rope-like tentacles started snaking their way through the bed, elbowing out the cringing campanula, the panic stricken penstemons and the petrified petunias. With mounting horror I watched impotently as these boa constrictors thickened and small pumpkins emerged. Gratified with his successful husbandry, the Assistant Gardener cavorted delightedly around the bed as he made plans for the largesse to be harvested. It was not to be: storm clouds gathered one afternoon and a hailstorm smashed the incipient pumpkins - ropes and all. His gardening ardor drastically dampened, the Assistant Gardener threw in the trowel. "To hell with it," he growled grumpily. His sunny disposition and winning smile returned only after being plied with several nice cups of tea and a few cream scones. Tea and sympathy worked its magic.

Be fruitful and multiply (Genesis) applies to perennials; annuals on the other hand complete their entire life cycle in one year, focusing all their energy into making seeds, which is why deadheading is important in prolonging the flowering period; if left to go to seed the plants will wither and die. While the blooming period of a perennial is three or four weeks, annuals bloom more quickly and for a longer time than any other plant. Although their stay in the garden is ephemeral, while it lasts it is brilliant.

Annuals are indispensable as fillers between perennials; the riot of color of the early and mid-season perennials will change to a lacklustre jumble if annuals are not used to fill in the gaps. The introduction of several patches of vivid annuals such as mid-size marigolds and cosmos, and the taller *Rudbeckia hirta* adds sparkle until the next wave of perennials starts blooming. Shorter annuals such as blue or purple *Lobelia erinus*, alyssum (*Lobularia maritima*) and the humble dwarf marigold adds edging interest.

A common mistake beginners make is planting tender annuals before the soil and climate are warm enough. Most warm climate annuals would resent being taken from their cozy nursery environment and placed in cold soil with perhaps frosty weather in the offing. All nursery bought annuals should be hardened off for a few days before being planted. Another surprising mistake is planting shade loving plants in full sun and vice versa. While

Left:
Whether planted in large or small containers, alyssum (*Lobularia maritima*) always makes a big splash of dazzling white. The individual flowers are modest, but if planted en masse, they will form a tight mat which will spill over the container in a pretty cascade.

Alyssum is inclined to go to seed if the weather is too hot and dry. To deal with this, they should be sheared, and within a month they will recover and continue to bloom prolifically.

begonias can take some sun, impatiens (busy Lizzie) in full sun would cease her scurrying; she would faint from exhaustion. Certain annuals such as portulaca and California poppy prefer dryer conditions; they are ideal Xeriscape plants.

If perennials are the batter of the cake, then annuals are the icing which tops the delicious confection. Good, friable soil is the most important part of the recipe. Dig the bed well - twelve inches or more - and remove all grass and weeds. Use copious amounts of peat, cow manure and compost. Dig again, making sure that all clumps of soil are broken up. Economizing on compost would be like leaving out the eggs or sugar in a recipe. Just as the batter of the cake must be well beaten, so too must the bed be well dug. Rake the bed, water thoroughly, then leave the soil to settle for a few days.

Above and right:
Lobelia erinus has a wonderful range of blue colors; sky-blue, dark blue, lilac and violet/purple. It is an easy annual to grow, for its wants are few—sun/part shade and moderate water. The intense colors combine well with white, pink or yellow edging plants. A small area devoted entirely to this plant is a stunning sight. If conditions are too dry or hot, lobelia tends to stop blooming. The remedy is a short haircut and increased moisture. The cascading varieties 'Sapphire' and the 'Regatta' series are indespensible for window boxes and hanging baskets.

Left:
Impatiens

Below:
Alyssum
begonias,
impatiens,
grass ,
*Rhynchelytrum
neriglume*
'Pink Chrystals'

Above:
Cosmos bipinnatus (Mexican aster) and zinnias fill in gaps in a perennial bed

A question frequently asked is whether fresh manure can be used to enrich the soil. A friend living near a dairy farm was offered the manure by her kind neighbor. Not wanting to look a gift cow in the mouth (or indeed any other unsavory part of the quadruped's anatomy), she accepted gratefully. The result was a fine crop of weeds in her pristine beds and plants burned by the strong smelling donation. The correct method is to add the manure to your compost heap, keeping it damp and constantly turned. While this method is not to be sniffed at, I find it easier to buy bags of weed-free compost and manure.

For a simple bed which requires little designing, petunias, (natives of Argentina), are hard to beat. Their range of colors is spectacular and they will bloom until frost. However, they do have an enemy, the wretched budworm. This irritating invertebrate is the plague of petunias, *Pelargoniums* (geraniums) and snapdragons. Why the moth lays its eggs in these flowers is a "mythtery" or perhaps a "mothtery"; the damage they do is frustrating. If one looks closely at the affected plant one can see the worm cleverly camouflage itself into whichever color flower it is dining on. Small holes appear in the buds and fine black droppings can be seen on the flower and greenery; this heralds the unwelcome return of the annoying pest. A radical method is to pinch off all the buds; otherwise a commercial spray can be used.

If the bed is wide enough, six feet or more, a background of greenery, small shrubs such as daphne, boxwood or the shorter spiraea, will provide a contrast against which the annuals will glow.

Opposite page:
Above:
Gloriosa daisy (*Rudbeckia hirta*)

Below:
Petunias

Right:
Portulaca grandiflora (Moss rose), verbena

The following are some combinations of annuals which are easy to maintain, and which have the most visual appeal.

1. Incorporating grasses into an annual bed is dramatic and unusual. Background clumps of *Stipa tenuissima* (ponytail grass) have delicate foliage and silky graceful waving plumes, or rhynchelytrum nerviglume "Pink Chrystals," a new introduction from the Denver Botanic Gardens and Colorado State University, has shimmering plumes of ruby and silver. Either of these grasses with drifts of pale and deep pink petunias or lilac, blue and purple petunias would delight and satisfy the longing for color and contrast.

2. White flowers add sparkle to a bed, for they combine well with any color. A simple yet effective bed giving months of pleasurable viewing would be pink and white medium-sized cosmos 'Sonata'. A fringe of *Lobelia erinus* or alyssum is a charming contrast. Cosmos mix amiably with most other plants and the feathery foliage adds to its appeal.

3. A beguiling combination is the stately cleome (spider flower) as a background, the middle of the bed filled with tall and mid-size snapdragons, and a frill of purple verbena (tapiens) in the front.

4. Masses of tall disease-resistant zinnias at the back, with the rest of the bed filled with marigolds 'Orange lady' would be considered a "hot" bed and while eye-catching might not be to the taste of nervous gardeners.

5. Though their season is short, California poppies with their intense yellow color glow in a bed; however they seed themselves prolifically and become a nuisance, and when push comes to shovel we don't want them to overrun the garden. Selective thinning is the answer, and when they become unattractively stringy, usher them out. I remove them at the end of June and re-plant the bed. It is not without a struggle that we part company, they protest all the way to the garbage bag. Self sown cosmos should be thinned out, too; the flowers will be bigger and the plant will be healthier.

6. For those who grow vegetables, annuals should not be overlooked, for they can be grown together success fully. The potager dates back to medieval times and is a harmonious blend of vegetable and annuals; it is a feast for the eyes as well as the appetite. Who could resist the sight of vibrant beds of lettuce and beets hobnobbing with dahlias or petunias, the feathery foliage of carrots living cheek by jowl with marigolds? *Nicotiana alata* (flowering tobacco) or heliotrope would add fragrance to the merry mélange. For those gardeners who work full time or who have small children to care for, an annual bed is the ideal way to provide a patch of color to brighten an otherwise dreary vista. Without having to expend a great deal of time, energy or money, annuals are the fastest way to achieve color. Within a week or two of being planted, they will obligingly unfurl a few flowers which will whet the appetite for the mouthwatering show to come. At the end of the season and in the gloom of winter one can sigh, "The annuals have ended, but the memory lingers on."

Right:
California poppies
(*Eschscholzia californica*) in planter

Below:
California poppies in planter
replaced at the end of June
by begonias

Opposite page:
Cosmos 'Sonata,' *Lobelia erinus*

107

A Small Flagstone Planter

The appearance of the flat, narrow space bordering my neighbor's property, was considerably improved by installing a small flagstone planter in the middle of the narrow perennial bed. By raising the level, this center-piece, planted with annuals, nicely balances the tall perennials flanking it. What had been an otherwise dull expanse, has become, with the addition of the planter, a charming focal feature. Compared to the difficulties I encountered when designing the back garden, I found that building the planter was a piece of cake.

1. A 6 inch deep trench was dug the length of the property line behind the perennial bed.

2. Railroad ties were laid in the trench, then a second row was laid on top of them.

3. Marking the place where the planter was to begin and end, a third row of ties was placed in that section.

4. Narrow flagstone pieces were laid in a semi-circle in the front of the three tiers of ties. The flagstone pieces
   were built up until they reached the level of the top ties.

5. The planter was filled with a mix of good garden soil, top soil and compost. The soil was allowed to settle for a week, then more mix was added.

The soil in the planter should be refreshed every year by removing several inches of the soil, then adding more bags of compost and manure. These additions should be dug in before planting the annuals. There are areas in every garden where it would be impossible to have a bed. Tree roots, stony soil or difficult slopes are some of the obstacles preventing the gardener from enjoying a flower bed. A planter, if well placed, can be the solution to these problems. A small planter is the ideal spot in which to grow eye-catching annuals.

Chapter Eleven

A CUP OF TEA, A CUP OF TEA,
MY KINGDOM FOR A CUP OF TEA!

An English Tea

Family traditions are important. Passing down recipes and garden lore fosters a feeling of security and solidarity. If one generation casts aside these customs, they are lost forever, and a link in the chain of the family's history is broken.

One of the traditions inherited from the British Empire is afternoon tea. Throughout the Empire, the ceremony was unchanging. It continues to be enjoyed today in all the Commonwealth countries.

During the Victorian and Edwardian periods, afternoon tea evolved to bridge the gap between lunch and dinner. It nicely filled the interval between the two meals for those of the leisured classes who became peckish in the late afternoon. The aristocracy gathered in the drawing room or library for this elegant affair. Up until the First World War, ladies changed into fashionable tea gowns. The middle classes soon adopted this custom (though without the tea gowns). It was a civilized way to entertain friends.

Tea - Camellia sinensis — became popular in England among the aristocracy in the seventeenth century with the return of the exiled King Charles the Second and his Portuguese Queen, Catherine of Braganza. Earlier, tea had arrived in Portugal and Holland from China. The Chinese had invented and had been using porcelain teapots and tea cups for centuries before the Europeans imported them. In the Regency and Victorian periods, exquisite sterling silver tea services were wrought by fine silversmiths in Britain. Plated silver soon followed, allowing those of more modest means to enjoy the same elegance. In England, in the nineteenth century, the pottery firm of Spode was the first to discover the formula for "bone" china, a mixture of bone ash and clay.

Other potteries throughout Europe and America soon followed suit, producing the beautiful china with which we are familiar today.

These treasures—china, delicate linens, and silverware—should be cherished as they pass from one generation to the next. They should also be used, for what benefit are they to anyone if they're locked away in a cupboard?

High tea was the Victorian working man's early supper. The men worked long hours in the factories and mines, and when they came home, they expected an early, substantial meal accompanied by their favorite brew—tea. This early supper consisted of, for example, shepherd's pie, sausages, steak and kidney pie, as well as wedges of home made bread. Fruit tarts rounded off the meal with a final "cuppa." Seated around the kitchen table, grandparents, parents and children would partake of this delicious feast, with the mother presiding over the teapot, which was replenished many times.

Opposite page and this page:
Tea in the garden

The difference in the varieties of tea is determined by the region in which it is grown. At higher altitudes, the quality of the tea is superior, because, in the cooler air, the leaves mature more slowly. The tips of the new season's growth are considered the best, and they are more expensive.

- ◆ Black (fermented) teas are grown in Sri Lanka, formerly Ceylon, and in Darjeeling, India.

- ◆ Earl Grey tea was named for the second Earl, who brought it back from China in the nineteenth century. It is a blend of Darjeeling and China teas, and is scented with oil of bergamot, a citrus fruit.

- ◆ Oolong teas are a blend of black and green teas.

- ◆ Green teas are unfermented and are the most delicate of all. They are never served with milk.

Great fortunes were made by the firms importing this valuable commodity. The most famous is Twinings, whose history goes back centuries.

Making a pot of tea is a simple procedure.

1. Fill a tea kettle with water and bring it to a boil.

2. Fill the teapot with hot water to warm it, then empty it.

3. If using loose tea, measure one teaspoon per person, and one extra for the pot. A strainer should be used when pouring this tea. If using tea bags , allow one per person.

4. Pour the boiling water into the teapot, and let it steep for several minutes.

The host always makes and pours the tea for the guests, who should be asked beforehand whether milk or a lemon slice is preferred. Whether to add the milk before or after pouring is a matter of taste. A teaspoon of sugar added to the cup further enhances the flavor. If the tea party is large, the host should ask one or two friends to help with the pouring.

Small children love tea parties. Dressed in their best clothes, the children's manners are usually impeccable, for even the youngest are aware that they are participating in a special, formal occasion.

Tea on the patio

The sandwich — a filling between two slices of bread — was named for the Earl of Sandwich in the eighteenth century, who, legend has it, was unwilling to leave the gaming table when dinner was served. This novel idea soon became wildly popular.

Cucumber sandwiches — a staple of tea parties — made from thinly sliced bread (crusts removed, then cut into fingers, squares or triangles), and scones with jam and cream, are easy to assemble. For a more lavish spread, meringues with whipped cream and strawberries, Madeira cake or English trifle could be added. Many people don't have the time to bake. Pastries bought from a good bakery are perfectly acceptable, especially when these dainties are arranged attractively on a lovely plate.

A tea party is less expensive and time consuming than having a dinner party. It is also more relaxing for you and your friends. All that is needed is a table covered with crisp linen or tablemats, a simple arrangement of fresh flowers, good china and gleaming silverware. In the summer, what could be more pleasant than a tea party in the garden, on the patio or on an apartment balcony? The open air sharpens the appetite, and a hot cup of tea is surprisingly refreshing.

The host should have everything ready fifteen minutes before the arrival of the first guests. A harried and red-faced host dashing back and forth does not bode well for creating a tranquil atmosphere. When the guests arrive, the thoughtful host should make sure that everyone is introduced; each guest should be made to feel welcome.

For a formal tea, the guests should be seated comfortably, whether it is at a table set for four, six or eight. It is useful to have a small table or trolley nearby on which to keep the scones, cakes, extra lemon slices and milk. The sandwiches are passed around first, to be followed by the scones and the cake. If there is room on the table, these plates should be left for guests to help themselves, otherwise they can be returned to the serving table. Fruit such as cherries or strawberries in a small bowl, or fresh fruit salad ladeled into pretty glasses would add to the carefree summer feeling.

An attentive host will make sure that empty tea cups are re-filled promptly. In an atmosphere such as this, who could fail to enjoy a tea party?

Inviting our friends, men and women, to a tea party, whether formal or informal, lets them know their friendship is valued; by taking the time to provide them with a simple, traditional, and elegant setting, our desire to please them will be obvious and our efforts will be appreciated.

SCONES

3/4 - 1 Cup self-rising flour
pinch of salt
1/2 stick or 4 tablespoons margarine or butter
1/2 cup or slightly more of milk
Preheat oven 425°

Rub butter or margarine into the dry ingredients
until it becomes coarse.
Add milk and mix with a fork.
Add more milk if necessary - dough should not be
too dry.
Turn onto a floured board (don't handle dough
too much).
Sprinkle the top with more flour, flatten to about
1 inch thick, then cut into rounds.
Place on cookie sheet and bake 12-15 minutes on
the second shelf from the bottom of the oven.
Yield, six scones.

TRIFLE

1 small sponge or pound cake
Raspberry and Peach Jam
1 Cup chopped walnuts or pecans
1/2 cup of sherry, 2 tablespoons brandy

Cut the cake into thick slices. Sandwich half
of them together with the raspberry jam, the
other half with peach jam. Slice them into
fingers and line the bottom and the sides of
a glass bowl with some of the fingers, arranging
them so that the jam filling shows through
the bowl. Sprinkle with half the nuts and
half the sherry and brandy.

Repeat until three quarters of the bowl is filled.

Next make the custard to be poured over the
trifle.

CUSTARD (for Trifle)

2 cups milk
1/2 cup sugar
3 large eggs
1/2 teaspoon vanilla
1 - 2 cups heavy cream for topping
Fresh raspberries

In a saucepan heat the milk with the sugar, stirring, until it is hot (do not boil). In a bowl beat the eggs well, then add the hot milk in a stream, stirring constantly. Transfer back to saucepan and cook over moderate heat, stirring, approximately 8 minutes. Do not boil. As soon as bubbles appear remove from the heat. Stir in the vanilla. Cool, then strain over cake in glass bowl. Chill, covered for at least 3 hours or overnight. Before serving, beat the cream until it holds stiff peaks and cover the top of the trifle. Sprinkle with nuts, and garnish with the fruit. Glaceed or canned fruit can be substituted for fresh fruit. Yield 6-8 servings.

MERINGUE (individual)

3 Egg Whites
1 cup granulated sugar
Oven 150 - 200°

Beat egg whites until stiff, then gradually add sugar, one tablespoon at a time.
Beat constantly until mixture is very stiff.
On a cookie sheet or tin foil, drop one tablespoon of the mixture, leaving a few inches between each meringue.
Place on second shelf from the bottom of the oven for 1 - 2 hours. Check after one hour. When cool, sandwich together with stiffly beaten double cream and decorate with strawberries. Meringues will stay fresh for a week or more if stored in an air-tight container.
Yield, 12 meringues.

117

A SURE-FIRE WAY TO DETER GATECRASHERS

Chicken wire cages can be effective in protecting tulips and other bulbs from browsing deer. They are useful too, for deterring squirrels from digging up newly planted bulbs. In the past, before the cages were made, when I planted bulbs in the fall, I would have an uneasy feeling of being watched by these clever little creatures as they scampered through the trees. The following morning my worst fears would be confirmed, as grinding my teeth in rage, I viewed the damage.

In certain areas of Denver, ravenous rabbits can make vegetable gardening difficult. Gardeners have to wage an unceasing and usually fruitless battle in order to protect their crops. Several of these cages placed over medium sized vegetables (the cages securely anchored with edging pins) would protect them. As the cages are light, they could be removed when weeding has to be done.

CHAPTER TWELVE

I LOOKED OUT THE WINDOW AND TO MY SURPRISE,
I SAW A DEER OF TREMENDOUS SIZE.
IT WAS WELL FED AND SLEEK, IT HAD QUITE A GIRTH,
IT ATE ALL MY TULIPS - $200 DOLLARS WORTH

The Gatecrashers

Planning garden beds is similar to planning a large party. The setting is right, and the weather looks as though it will co-operate; all that needs to be done is to invite the guests. Combing through your list you will have chosen the most amiable and interesting of your friends and relatives. However, because of circumstances beyond your control, you find yourself having to invite your best friend's cousin, she's the one with the purple hair and pierced body parts, who not only drinks herself under the table, but sometimes under several guests as well. To avoid hurt feelings, Aunt Edith's doddering brother has to be included. Uncle Howie's interminable stories of his camping trip to Dry Gulch Park, Nevada, can empty a room faster than your sister-in-law's offer to sing some arias from Aida. These guests may be unwelcome, but they are invited. It's the gatecrashers who are the problem – people you've never met who arrive because a friend told them that they'd be an asset at the party. In my garden, the welcome guests are the roses, clematis, perennials and annuals. The gatecrashers are certain birds, slugs and deer; added to this dreary list are the weeds, those ruffians of the garden.

Birds are our feathered friends, but too many of them can be a problem. Several years ago several dozen bluish black birds rejoicing in the name of grackles, took up residence in the garden; it was an invasion. The musical twitterings of the other birds were drowned out by the harsh squawks of the interlopers. Their iridescent coats gleaming in the sun, these odious creatures strutted around, diving and swooping menacingly if anyone approached their nests. The neighborhood was under siege. They attacked joggers and passersby, they intimidated dogs, they even frightened a little old lady on her leisurely walk.

Unable to relax in my once peaceful garden, I appealed to my Protector and Better Half, the Assistant Gardener. Having fortified himself with several strong cups of tea, he donned an overcoat (to protect his body), a pair of skiers goggles (to protect his eyes), and a cowboy hat (to protect his head). The temperature outside was 90 degrees. Arming himself with
a stout stick and twirling umbrella, he sallied
forth to do battle. Initially the birds were
taken aback by this apparition, so that under
cover of the umbrella I was able to deadhead
an entire bed. Then they attacked, setting up
such a din of clacking and screeching, their
cronies from far and wide flew in to help.
Their swooping was so unnerving the
Assistant Gardener and I were forced to
make a strategic withdrawal. Alfred
Hitchcock would have rejoiced at the scene.
Sweating profusely, the Protector disrobed,
then retired behind his newspaper. "To hell
with them," he muttered disgustedly.

A week later, to everyone's relief, the birds
flew away. Peace and harmony were
restored and everyone could return to their
normal routines:

Teenagers on motorized scooters could once
more roar aimlessly up and down the street.;
Chuckling babies could be wheeled with
impunity on the sidewalk; Canines could
resume their sniffing and squirting activities.

The following year there was a mysterious
decrease in the numbers of grackles; they also were less aggressive. The colder winter weather might have been the reason for this change, or perhaps the arrival of several hawks dampened their enthusiasm for our area.

Slugs will chew their way through a bed of annuals in a week. These horrible hermaphrodites (they fertilize each other's eggs), come out at night and they are most prevalent after it rains. Their eggs can overwinter and in spring they emerge to decimate any new growth. They become dormant in hot, dry weather but as soon as conditions cool, they will copulate enthusiastically and lay more eggs. To deal with them, I go out at dusk with my trusty scissors, and emulating Henry the Eighth, decapitate as many of them as possible. There are poisons which are effective, but unfortunately they can harm small animals, birds and children; I prefer to use beer. Soda cans cut in half then filled partially with the liquid works safely and efficiently. Each morning when I inspect the cans and find dozens of corpses, I rub my hands with glee and dance my way around the beds. Some gardeners make their own effective mixture of water, sugar and baker's yeast; it's the yeasty smell that lures the slugs to their doom.

Deer are charming creatures, but they used to wreak havoc in my spring garden, devouring hundreds of tulips, as well as the buds of the early blooming perennials. I tried everything—mothballs, soap and commercial sprays—nothing worked. A friend told me that allowing chewing tobacco to steep overnight in a container, then straining it and pouring it on the plants would be a deterrent. Early the next morning, I scurried to the convenience store and asked in my rather high-pitched, squeaky voice for a dozen packets of chewing tobacco and two six packs of beer (for the slugs).

Dogs stopped barking, strong men paled and a leather-jacketed teenager gaped. Clutching a bag of dough-nuts, Twinkies™ and a large Slurpy™, a tubby woman in abbreviated shorts paused interestedly at the exit. She shifted a wad of gum from one side of her mouth to the other and sniggered.

The clerk cleared his throat, breaking the deathly hush. He gazed at me speculatively. "Lady," he shook his head reproachfully, "you've got some bad habits there". My agitated denials and confused explanations were met with skepticism and a broad wink. "Uh huh," he smirked incredulously. "well, hell lady, I reckon we all have our problems." Chastened and red-faced, I crept out of the store with my purchases.

I have been back to that store, but not without first donning my Groucho Marx disguise. The potent cocktail worked well because I also added hot chili powder to the mix. When dealing with gatecrashers, the Marquess of Queensberry rules can be ignored.

Further protection for the tulips is provided by sturdy cages made from chicken wire and steel tubing. The cages, (made by a handyman), measure five feet by three feet and are three feet high. Each cage encloses approximately 40 tulips, the cages being placed over the newly planted bulbs in late October. Edging pins anchor the cages which are removed when the tulips are about to bloom in spring. This is the time the foothills turn green providing the deer with an abundance to eat. I continue spraying the emerging perennials with the tobacco mixture, paying special attention to the tempting new foliage of the roses.

I try to garden as naturally as possi-ble. I avoid using poisons, preferring to let nature take its course. Plants that are susceptible to diseases or pests are replaced quickly with their hardier brethren.

Gardening can give one so much plea-sure; the setbacks and frustrations are more than com-pensated for by the successes and the feeling of accom-plishment as one views a lovely bed.

Weeds

A weed-free, beautifully maintained bed of *Lobelia erinus* and begonias

Can there be a more depressing sight than a beautiful bed of flowers being overrun by ugly weeds? Gorgeous flowers having to hobnob with dandelions, aggressive grasses and bindweed is like a refined woman dressed in elegant clothes, being taken to dinner at what she thinks will be a stylish restaurant, but to her dismay, finds herself at a rough bar surrounded by drunken louts. Well-bred flowers deserve an appropriate setting and congenial companions.

Money spent on buying expensive flowers and the energy expended on preparing the bed will be wasted if the chore of weeding is neglected. Close planting can obviate the need for constant weeding, because if a space is left empty for even five minutes, the gardener's reward will be a healthy crop of thuggish and sometimes unidentifiable weeds. Combating these hooligans before they can establish themselves requires constant digging and turning of the soil in spring. After the bed has been planted, use the points of a scissor or a sturdy screwdriver to dig out emerging grasses or shallow-rooted weeds.   Desultory weeding is useless; breaking or scraping off the tops of the weeds will strengthen their roots, so that by the middle of summer the disheartening result will be tall, healthy weeds under which the gardener can relax on a chaise longue.

Perennials, as they spread and grow taller, can deprive most weeds of light and air. The exception is the pernicious bindweed which winds itself coyly around defenseless plants. Trying to dig them out can be frustrating, as their roots seem to reach into the very bowels of the earth. Half-hearted digging will cause the roots to regenerate, therefore, the only recourse is repeated deep digging. If all else fails, a systemic weedkiller might have to be used to solve the problem. This weedkiller is carried from the leaves through the plant to the roots. It is effective in eradicating persistent and deep-seated weeds. Although I dislike using chemical weedkillers, in extreme cases it is the only method for ridding a bed of these twining horrors. Always wear rubber gloves and protective clothing when handling and applying weedkiller, and follow the instructions carefully. Protect plants and shrubs nearby by covering them with plastic bags. Never use the spray when it is windy or when rain is imminent. A safer method than spraying is to use a paintbrush or a rag soaked in the liquid. The whole weed can be coated without the danger of contaminating valuable plants.

If a large, uncultivated area is being contemplated as a future flowerbed but weeds and grasses are a problem, an easy though unsightly method to eradicate them is to cover the entire area with an old carpet or plastic bags weighted down.

Plants brought from the nursery should be checked for weeds before being planted. As our gardens are full of our own thriving weeds, it's unnecessary to swell their ranks by introducing visitors. Like "The Man Who Came To Dinner" they might settle in happily and never leave.

Chapter Thirteen

LATIN IS A DEAD LANGUAGE,
AS DEAD AS DEAD CAN BE,
IT KILLED THE ANCIENT ROMANS
AND NOW IT'S KILLING ME

Odds and Ends . . . Bits and Pieces

 sing botanical names is important, because without them the gardening world would become like the Tower of Babel. Common names can vary widely from region to region; Latin is the unifying language, the Esperanto of the horticultural community. Making the effort to study and remember botanical names can have benefits, such as when you're in a group of frighteningly erudite and knowledgeable gardeners, how lightly "Helenium autumnale" trips off your tongue. It beats "sneezeweed" hands down.

The following are some suggestions for garden pests and disasters. My apologies to Latin scholars for mangling a beautiful language.

Slugs - Sluggae horribilis

Deer - Deerae aggravatium

Unleashed dogs - Caninae urinus et turdius maxima

Hail - Aqua freezium devastatium

Re-action of Gardeners Viewing Damage - Exasperatus in extremis, Holy #%@%!! maxissima

Tips

- Chicken wire is useful for providing support for clematis and annual vines. It also can be used as an emergency covering to deter deer from nibbling at perennial spring growth. Position the wire over the vulnerable plants and secure it with edging pins. Ask the hardware store to cut the wire into manageable lengths, because if the roll is too long, trying to cut it with a (usually) blunt secatur becomes a Sisyphean test of endurance as the roll keeps springing back. I have been trapped in an unwieldy roll which stubbornly refused to stay flat. My weak cries for help were answered by my chivalrous Consort/Assistant Gardener who galloped to the rescue. Had it not been for him my skeletal remains would still be decorating the driveway. Wear gloves when handling chicken wire, the cut edges are sharp.

- Mint grown in a bed can be invasive. Grow it in a wide concrete pipe or flue which has been sunk two feet into the soil. Thus contained, the roots won't spread. Another solution is to grow this wonderful herb in a barrel or a large pot.

- Tie a brightly colored ribbon around your small implements. If you drop them in the lawn they'll be easy to find.

- Weeds in sidewalk cracks can be eradicated by dissolving a cup of salt in two quarts of boiling water. Pour the boiling liquid onto the weeds, but be careful not to let any run into your beds.

- Caveat emptor! Be cautious when you see the words vigorous or fast growing to describe groundcovers. These are euphemisms for plants which are intent on taking over the world. Dynamite might be the only option when you try to get rid of them. Even after ruthless eradication they will peek out at you from unexpected places.

- Two or three tulips huddled together look pathetic. Be generous by planting eight or ten in a group; these will have a greater visual impact.

- If you neglected to stake some floppy perennials, make a "corset". Place four stout sticks around the plant, then starting at the bottom wind the string firmly around the sticks until it ends at the top. This treatment can be effective; it's better than doing nothing but watch the plants keel over during windy weather.

- Mowing the lawn with a manual mower is excellent excercise; it is also good for the environment. As it has no catcher, it is light and easy to operate. The clippings left on the lawn provide nutrients.

- One set each of scissors, hedgecutters, garden fork and gloves should be kept in the front and back garden. This will save you having to rush around when chores have to be taken care of in either area.

- Make an inventory of your tools. Get rid of handleless rakes or bent forks, because two prongs won't dig it right.

. . . And Bits and Pieces

You're a committed gardener if you:
Go to a glamorous cocktail party, and the only interesting person there to talk to is a little old lady who knows the difference between achillea filipendulina and achillea millefolium.

Set out to buy groceries, then for some unaccountable reason find yourself in the nursery parking lot.

Visit friends and relatives and the trunk of your car is filled with emergency supplies of scissors, secaturs, string, chicken wire and half a bag of compost.

Can sleep through your spouse's snoring but you're instantly alert when you hear deer munching on your tulips.

Go to the nursery with the firm resolve not to buy but to "browse," then to your surprise, find yourself at the check-out counter with a cart filled to the brim with plants.

Welcome to the wonderful world of gardening.

We all have our foibles and eccentricities, silly economies like collecting odd lengths of string, hoarding used gift wrap, and re-using tin foil. My Significant Other and Assistant Gardener, while usually generous to a fault, hates to waste plastic garbage bags. In the fall, when I cut down the perennials and generally put the garden to bed, he will stand guard over the bags to make sure that they are filled to the brim.

He goes about this task scientifically, cutting the stalks into neat pieces, then stacking them in the bag. Every now and then, he thrusts his foot, encased in a size 13 shoe, into the bag, firmly tamping down the contents.

"There," he will say triumphantly, as the bag starts to split, "I could fit another whole bed into this bag.

This jubilance is premature as the bag is so heavy, a forklift is needed to lift it. In the absence of this useful piece of machinery, he drags the bag the length of the garden, scattering debris in his wake. He deposits it in the driveway, where it finally bursts. Undeterred, he will transfer the contents to two more bags. He is convinced that this method saves bags.

His other quirk is searching through the advertisements looking for bargains. The words "Sale" and "Discount" make his eyes sparkle.

El Cheapo Nursery and Garden Supply. 50% off! Terra Cotta Pots, (chipped & slightly irregular). Hurry while supplies last!

My argument that we have enough chipped pots of our own falls on deaf ears, for he's studying the next piece of literature. It is sprinkled with excited exclamation points.

Big John's U Fixit & Hardware Store.
Hurry to Big John's for BIG SAVINGS!!!

Mowers (wheels need fixing, fuel tanks slightly dented) 75% off!!!

First ten customers win FREE trip to Monster Truck Rally in Alabama!!!

But who am I to talk? Hidden in a closet, in the bowels of the house, is a basket overflowing with eight miles of salvaged, irregular lengths of string.

Chapter Fourteen

FOOLS RUSH IN WHERE WARY GARDENERS FEAR TO TREAD

Steps, Centerpieces, Circles and Shrubs

 gentle slope can be a valuable asset, as it is an ideal place to build steps. These would make a strong, central statement as well as dividing the garden into different areas.

Because a large, featureless area can look boring, steps can offer an opportunity to add interest to a garden design. Even in a small area, a note of drama can be introduced by installing two or three steps. These need not be ornate, for a few well constructed steps can be as effective as a complicated design. They should harmonize with the overall plan of the garden. Wide, shallow steps are more graceful; they induce the viewer to pause and then want to explore further. Narrow, steep steps, on the other hand, look less inviting; they can also be more dangerous to negotiate. The rise of each step should be four to six inches, while the tread should be at least twelve to fourteen inches deep. In a plain garden, steps flanked by pots or urns can be the main architectural feature. Homeowners who are starting a new garden have a clean slate on which to work, for they have the advantage of being able to incorporate several steps or other pleasing features into their plans.

Above: Squares of grass were removed and flagstone was inserted in its place.
Below: Various thymes enliven the steps

Above: *Coreopsis verticillata* 'Zagreb' and thyme
Below: Lemon thyme (*Thymus x citriodorus*) and red creeping thyme (*Thymus coccineus*)

Centerpieces

For an eye-catching display, a small shrub or perennial as a centerpiece in a container is hard to beat. They are effective whether they are surrounded by a cluster of pots, or lined up along a path. The centerpiece may overwinter if watered and given adequate protection. However, I remove mine and replant them in the beds in late fall.

Above Right:
Hosta x undulata (Plantain Lily)

Below right:
dwarf Alberta spruce

Opposite page:
Above left:
dwarf Alberta spruce

Above right:
Privet

Below left:
Buxus (boxwood)

Below right:
Rhychelytrum nerviglume
'Pink Chrystals'

Circles

Some gardeners object to planting around trees; they feel that this could damage the trees, but I have planted around my Marshall ash trees for fifteen years, and have found no cause for alarm. Annuals such as *Lobelia erinus*, alyssum, begonias and impatiens have shallow roots, which make deep digging unnecessary. Circles around trees are an easy way of adding color to an otherwise featureless stretch of lawn. Make a generous circle around the tree - a tiny circle looks silly and isn't worth the effort involved. The circle will look even sillier if the tree is large, rather like a giant perched on a mushroom.

Above: Alyssum, impatiens, *Lobelia erinus*

Below: Pansies (*V. wittrockiana*), begonias, *Lobelia erinus*

Shrubs

If you suffer from a lack of privacy in your back garden – forcing you to gaze either on the one side of your property at your neighbor (attired in his underwear), tinkering with his rattletrap vehicle, or on the other side, at the rickety shed erected several years previously, and lovingly added to yearly – then large shrubs are the answer to screening you from these disagreeable vistas. Well planned plantings of shrubs can create almost instant privacy, as well as softening bare walls. For those homeowners who haven't the time or energy to devote to a perennial bed, well selected evergreen and deciduous shrubs can provide year-long interest. They lend structure to a garden; they can also act as a noise barrier. As shrubs are permanent elements in the garden, the soil should be well prepared with additions of manure, compost and bone meal.

Evergreens

Above Left: Although pinyon (*Pinus edulis*) is a tree, I use it in my garden as a large shrub. Several of them are invaluable for creating a sense of enclosure. Heavy branching lends a rich appearance to them, and an added bonus is that they are drought tolerant. I prune mine to keep them to a manageable size, for in a small space they can overwhelm. In a larger space they should be allowed to reach their natural size.

Above Right: Rocky Mountain Juniper (*Juniperus scopulorum*) adds an elegant vertical touch to the garden. If well placed it can be a focal point of interest. It can also be pruned into whatever shape the gardener fancies; obelisk, pyramid, lollipop or slender column.

Above Left:

Spruce dwarf Alberta (*Picea glauca* 'Conica') needs no shearing, for this dense, formal shrub has a natural conical shape. It has bright green needles which are especially attractive in Spring. I can't help smiling when I look at this handsome evergreen because it looks so plump and pleased with itself. If possible, it should be planted in a more protected position. Several of these shrubs planted in a long border make a striking impression.

Above Right:

Arborvitae, (*Thuja occidentalis*) is a slow growing, emerald green beauty, whose textural contrast would complement any group of shrubs. The foliage is fine-textured, its flattened sprays resemble those of junipers. It is an ideal accent plant as well. For some unknown reason (and to my intense irritation), the deer love to nibble on this shrub. Every winter I have to enclose it in chicken wire to protect it. I use so much chicken wire in my garden, my Financial Backer/Assistant Gardener predicts that there will soon be a world-wide shortage of this useful commodity.

Deciduous

Above and Right:
There is no more breathtaking sight than a 'Snowball' bush (*Viburnum opulis sterilis* 'Roseum') in full bloom. It is festooned in early summer with huge balls of minute flowers - some as big as tennis balls. Initially they are green, but as they ripen, they turn a creamy white. This shrub is excellent for screening purposes, and if necessary, it can be pruned (immediately after flowering), to any desired height.

Below Right:
At a higher elevation, there is no better lilac to grow than 'Miss Kim' (*Syringa patula*) for she blooms several weeks after the other lilacs. The blossoms of the earlier lilacs can be ruined by an unexpected cold snap. In my garden 'Miss Kim' has been impervious to the vagaries of the weather; she has bloomed blithely every year.
What a winner!

Left:
There are ten tallhedge, buckthorn (*Rhamnus frangula* 'Columnaris') dotted around my garden. If left to their own devices, they will grow to fifteen feet; I prefer to shear them to a manageable six feet every ten days. Formal and dense, they add symmetry and dignity to any area.

Below:
Elder (*Sambucus canadensis*) flowers profusely in mid-summer. It covers itself in large panicles of dazzling white, followed by black fruit. Elder's one drawback is the brittleness of its stems. I prune it back in spring, and within a few weeks it obligingly puts out strong new growth.

CHAPTER FIFTEEN

FROM MAY TO SEPTEMBER, I TRY TO REMEMBER,
THOSE COMPLEX BOTANICAL NAMES,
OVER BOOKS I WILL PORE, TO TRY TO LEARN MORE,
IT'S ALL GONE BY THE END OF DECEMBER.

Seasons

Spring is the burgeoning season when trees and shrubs with their faint dusting of pale green come to life. Bulbs push upward towards the light, and soft growth emerges from the early perennials. Amongst the tangle of dead twigs and leaves, the buds of the clematis swell, and a tinge of green can be seen in the lawn. Spring is the optimistic season for the gardener – a time of renewal and excitement.

Mid-summer is the fulfilling season as the gardener's hopes and plans come to fruition. This is not the time to relax, for as each wave of perennials blooms and dies, the gardener must prune and deadhead constantly. This is the season when the gardener feels the most enthusiastic, and when remodeling plans are hatched.

Late summer is the season when the gardener can enjoy the final wave of perennials taking center stage. The annuals, as though sensing the change in the air, hurry to put out as many blooms as possible, for they know that their time is limited. The roses too, in this, their last flush, are at their most magnificent; their stems are heavy with buds waiting to open for their final burst of glory. The last of the clematis to bloom, "Sweet Autumn Clematis," drapes its dazzling white flowers over fences, a fitting finale to a successful season.

Spring

Left, above and below:
The tuber/corm of *Anemone coronaria* 'De Caen' is hard and raisin-like. It would seem unlikely that an exquisite flower could be produced from this unpromising looking, knobby object. Miraculously though, in Spring, parsley-like foliage emerges, followed by sturdy stems topped with plump buds. These unfurl to reveal glowing flowers with their velvet centers. If planted in generous groups, they will make showy splashes of red, purple, and mauve in the late spring/early summer. Their requirements are modest: moderately rich, well-drained soil, sun, with some afternoon shade. Before planting, I soak the tubers overnight in a bucket of water. Anemones are superb flowers for cutting.

Above:
Basket of gold
(*Aurinia saxatilis*)

Below:
Korean lilac
'Miss Kim,'
candy tuft
(*Iberis sempervirens*)

Tulips as Annuals

I have found over the years that treating tulips as annuals is a more sensible approach than having to look at their yellowing leaves for months after they have bloomed. Over time, the bulbs tend to drift into perennials and they keep popping up in unlikely places. It is also more difficult to dig and compost in a bed with bulbs scattered in it. After flowering, I remove all of the bulbs and re-plant the area in the fall with fresh supplies. The spaces vacated by the tulips can then be planted with summer annuals. Some people might consider this method wasteful. An aggrieved Assistant Gardener always looms over me tut-tutting his disapproval as the garbage bag fills with healthy looking bulbs. These objections fall on deaf ears. Experience has taught me that in my garden this method is by far the best. As Ingrid Bergman said to Walter Matthau in the move *Cactus Flower*, "you go to your church, I'll go to mine."

Right:
Darwin tulips 'Golden Parade'

Below:
Tulips 'Georgette'

Opposite page:
Above:
Tulips 'Georgette'
Anemone coronaria 'De Caen'

Below:
Darwin tulips

Foreground:
Tulips, Darwin mix,
Iberis sempervirens
(candytuft),
basket of gold
(*Aurina saxatilis*),
"lollipop" junipers

Background:
Pine, pinyon (*Pinus edulis*),
Colorado Blue Spruce
(*Picea pungens glauca*)

Mid-Summer

Left: yarrow (*Achilea millefolium* 'Paprika')

Below: Pinks (*Dianthus, d. x alwoodii, d. x deltoides*)

Opposite page:
'Ville de Lyon' clematis, pots of marguerite (*Anthemis tinctoria*) and *Lobelia erinus*, Jupiter's beard

Following pages:
Left page: cosmos, zinnias, black-eyed Susan, Beard tongue (*Penstemon*)

Right page:
Above: *Aster x frikartii*, black-eyed Susan, *Helenium autumnale*, begonias, alyssum, "lollipop" juniper

Below: alyssum (*Lobularia maritima*)

Obedient plant (*Physostegia virginiana* - false dragonhead), is an indispensible perennial for providing late-summer color. Two or three feet tall, its leaves are lance
shaped and it has deep pink or white spikes at the end of sturdy stems. It is a dignified plant, never sprawling unbecomingly over its neighbors. If given good soil and
regular watering, physostegia will bloom prolifically. However, under optimum conditions and too much water, it will spread and become invasive. It should be divided every two years to avoid becoming a nuisance. Every year I look forward to its
flowering period when the remarkably tame hummingbirds hover intently over the
snapdragon-like blooms. It prefers sun with some shade, and is hardy and disease-
resistant. It is an excellent cut flower.

Opposite page: grass *Rhynchelytrum nerviglume* 'Pink Crystals,' *Aster x frikartii, cosmos, rudbeckia hirta*, alyssum

Above: Lambs' Ears (*Stachys byzantina*), alyssum, *Sedum spectabile* 'Autumn Joy,'
obedient plant (*Physostegia virginiana*)
Below: *Asters novae-angliae* 'Alma Potschke,' 'Hella Lacy'

Opposite page:
Above: Obedient plant (*Physostegia virginiana*), black-eyed Susan
Below: *Asters novi-belgii* 'Winston Churchill,' 'Daniella,' alyssum, cosmos

One of the last perennials to bloom is *Sedum spectabile* 'Autumn Joy.' With its sturdy stems, fleshy leaves, and flat-topped clusters of pink flowerheads, it is a plant to be cherished. It behaves with uncommon civility in that it never infringes on its neighbor's space. It is disease-resistant and long-lived.

Fall

My neighbor's cottonwood tree (*Populis deltoides* 'Siouxland')
glows against a brilliant blue Colorado sky. In the foreground is a
Spruce (*Picea pungens glauca*, Colorado Blue spruce).

Winter

After the frantic pace of a busy summer season has ended, it's marvelous to be able to sit indoors and relax with books and a nice cup of tea. I love the winter, a snowstorm followed by days of sunshine and a brilliant Colorado blue sky. I can gaze out onto the garden, secure in the knowledge that the beds are tidy and composted, and that the tulips are protected under their chicken wire cages. I can wind my eight miles of salvaged string and the Assistant Gardener can count his plastic garbage bags. Who could ask for anything more?

Winter is the season for reflection. It is a time when the gardener can pause for a while and consider the season just passed and to contemplate the seasons yet to come. Unfortunately, it is also a time when the Assistant Gardener can focus all of his attention on the non-gardening items in the junk mail. These coupons put a smile on his face and a spring in his step.

"GRANPA'S PIZZA & CHILI PARLOR"
Buy 6 pizzas, get one bowl of HOT chili FREE!!   Hot & Spicy FREE!!

(From Denver, take highway 196 going North. Go approx. 80 miles & exit at Pete's Scrap Metal. Make a right onto dirt road, then veer left at Lurleen's Hot Spot Bar & Motel. Follow the arrows across railroad tracks to:

GRANPA'S FOR THE BEST PIZZA IN OUR GREAT STATE!
(Next to Honest Al's Auto Salvage)

And
"HAPPY GUMS & TEETH CLINIC"
Dr. Hank Conman D.D. & B.S.
(Swamplands Great Snake Community College, ARK)

PAINLESS EXTRACTIONS!!   BUY ONE SET OF DENTURES, GET ONE FREE!!
HURRY WHILE SUPPLY LASTS!   ALL EXTRACTIONS GUARANTEED!
FREE CANDY FOR YOU AND THE KIDS!!

When I point out mildly that we both have our own healthy sets of teeth, and that it was unlikely we would ever be following those arrows across railroad tracks to Granpa's, he mutters darkly that you never know, those coupons might come in handy some day. They are added to the growing pile in a box in the garage.

While he sifts happily through his largesse, I smile quietly to myself, for I know that when the chaos of spring planting is over, and the garage is cleaned out, that "handy" box will mysteriously disappear.

January

In January, the gardener looks out on a bleak scene of bare trees and brown lawns, with little to do except pore over catalogs and to check every few days to see whether bulbs are showing signs of life. January is the perfect time to invite friends over for an indoor tea.

Hosting an indoor tea is a splendid antidote for curing the mid-winter blues. If some of the guests are gardeners, ideas, plans and notes for the coming season can be exchanged and debated.

Opposite page:
A formal tea in the dining room
Cucumber sandwiches, scones, chocolate cake

Above:
Tea for two in a cozy nook in the living room
Cucumber sandwiches, scones, meringue with cream and raspberries

ACKNOWLEDGMENTS:

Special thanks to:

Carl Anderson whose wise advice, encouragement and help were invaluable at all times.

Carol Core who, despite all of the constant changes made, managed to keep her head and her patience in designing and re-designing the book.

Evalyn McGraw, editor of Colorado Homes & Lifestyles Magazine, who kindly published several of the chapters as articles in the magazine.

Chip and Lee-Ann Krauss for the transcription of the text.

Tom Gillam of Native Nursery who installed all of the flagstone features, the steps and the walls. He and his good-natured team were always helpful and understanding when plans and designs were altered.

Diane Gemmill, Echter's Garden Center for her detailed preparation of the index and proofreading.

David Radman, Photo Lab Manager, King Soopers, for developing and enlarging the photographs.

Barbe Granica for editing and proofreading.

Pat Allen, consulting rosarian.

Some of the rhymes and sayings in the text and beneath the chapter headings are the author's original verse, others were modified from various sources: popular sayings, nursery rhymes, Shakespeare, John Donne, Dorothy Parker and the Bible.

These photographs were taken by the author at the following locations:

Index

By way of explanation all Latin and common names are in alphabetical order. Common names are in regular print and are followed by "see...*the Latin name.*" Only the first letter of the common name is capitalized unless a proper noun is part of the common usage. That word is then capitalized. If the Latin name and common name are the same , no common name is given. Varieties/cultivars are not generally mentioned on the common name lines.

Latin names are italicized - the genus is given first and the first letter is capitalized, this is followed by the species, sub-species, varieties and forms which appear in small, italicized letters. Cultivars (a form of species or a hybrid) are given capital initials, no italics and are set apart by single invertedcommas. Plants forming part of a group are given with capital initials but no italics or inverted commas (the only one being the De caen group in the anemones). On the Latin name lines, the common name follows the Latin name in parenthesis.

163